Chess Puzzles for Kids

Murray Chandler

OFF TO THE BEACH – PUZZLE 58

First published in the UK by Gambit Publications Ltd 2012
Reprinted 2016, 2021

ISBN-13: 978-1-906454-40-1
ISBN-10: 1-906454-40-X

DISTRIBUTION:
Worldwide (except USA): Central Books Ltd, 50 Freshwater Rd, Chadwell Heath, London RM8 1RX .
Tel +44 (0)20 8986 4854 Fax +44 (0)20 8533 5821.
E-mail: orders@Centralbooks.com

Gambit Publications Ltd, 27 Queens Pine, Bracknell, Berks RG12 0TL, England.
E-mail: info@gambitbooks.com
Website (regularly updated): www.gambitbooks.com

Edited by Graham Burgess
Typeset by John Nunn
Printed and bound by TJ Books Limited, Padstow, Cornwall, England

10 9 8 7 6 5 4 3

Dedication: To Claire, who always beats her phone on level 2.

Acknowledgements: Graham Burgess, Leonard McLaren, Helen Milligan, Judy Gao, Natasha Fairley, Nicole Tsoi, Bruce Pollard, John Francis and Grant Kerr.

Illustrations: Cindy McCluskey

Gambit Publications Ltd
Directors: Dr John Nunn GM, Murray Chandler GM, and Graham Burgess FM
German Editor: Petra Nunn WFM
Bookkeeper: Andrea Burgess

Contents

100 Chess Puzzles

Introduction

This is a chess puzzle book with a difference. As well as containing many challenging puzzles to solve, the positions have additionally been selected to illustrate many typical and recurring *themes* and *patterns*.

Learning to recognize standard patterns of chess pieces is a powerful way to improve your game. Once these basic attacking formations are grasped, they become building blocks – instantly helping you to create deeper and more complex combinations.

There is a huge range of amazing tactical patterns covered here, as this book is designed to expand upon my two existing volumes on tactics (*How to Beat Your Dad at Chess* and *Chess Tactics for Kids*). To my knowledge, there is no overlap – all of the 260+ puzzles given in this current book are original. A few *themes* pop by for a second viewing, but even these tend to come with a surprise new twist.

It has been a pleasure selecting these puzzles, mostly sourced from recent games, and a big thank you to the players who created such wonderful combinations. Whether you try to solve the puzzles, or prefer simply to read the book for pleasure, there is plenty here to inspire us all in our own games.

Murray Chandler

Fright Knight

Algebraic Notation

	a	b	c	d	e	f	g	h	
8	a8	b8	c8	d8	e8	f8	g8	h8	8
7	a7	b7	c7	d7	e7	f7	g7	h7	7
6	a6	b6	c6	d6	e6	f6	g6	h6	6
5	a5	b5	c5	d5	e5	f5	g5	h5	5
4	a4	b4	c4	d4	e4	f4	g4	h4	4
3	a3	b3	c3	d3	e3	f3	g3	h3	3
2	a2	b2	c2	d2	e2	f2	g2	h2	2
1	a1	b1	c1	d1	e1	f1	g1	h1	1
	a	b	c	d	e	f	g	h	

The chess notation used in this book is the simple, algebraic notation in use throughout the world. It can be learnt by anyone in just a few minutes.

As you can see from the chessboard above, the files are labelled a-h (going from left to right) and the ranks are labelled 1-8. This gives each square its own unique reference point. The pieces are described as follows:

Knight = ♘
Bishop = ♗
Rook = ♖
Queen = ♕
King = ♔

Pawns are not given a symbol. When they move, simply the *destination square* is given.

Typical additional symbols used in chess books:

Check	=	+		Good move	=	!
Double Check	=	++		Bad move	=	?
Capture	=	x		Interesting idea	=	!?
Castles kingside	=	0-0		Not recommended	=	?!
Castles queenside	=	0-0-0		Brilliant move	=	!!
Ch	=	Championship		Disastrous move	=	??

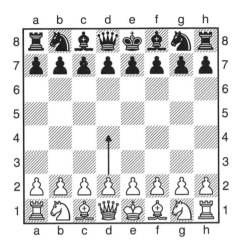

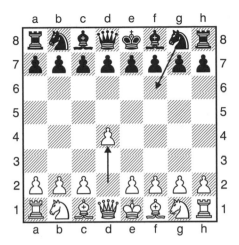

In the diagram above, White is about to play the move **1 d4**. The **1** indicates the move-number, and **d4** the destination square of the white pawn.

In this diagram, White's **1 d4** move is complete. Black is about to reply **1...♘f6** (moving his knight to the **f6-square** on his *first move*).

ARABIAN MATE

Using Puzzles to Improve

Solving chess puzzles is a fun way to get better at chess. The benefit is even greater if you are also learning – or reinforcing your knowledge of – *thematic chess patterns*. These chess patterns are familiar clusters of pieces and pawns, and they are great indicators that a certain tactic or combination might be possible.

All strong chess-players instinctively use pattern recognition to calculate tactical themes quicker and deeper. Even very simple themes and patterns can create some remarkable combinations when combined together.

The big advantage of recognizing patterns is that the knowledge can be used repeatedly, and in many different settings. As an example, let's have a look here at a single pattern – just one of many covered in this book. Although it is a checkmating formation of some ferocity, it doesn't even have an official name, so I have dubbed it a 'Mighty Mate' (see Puzzles 47 & 48).

The 'Mighty Mate' position given below was reached in an official tournament game. As is normal in chess books, the caption by the diagram identifies the players, the place and the date. The first-named player (Khantuev) is playing **White**, and the second-named player (Ivenin) had the **black** pieces. The game was played in the city of **Irkutsk**, Russia, in the year **2010**.

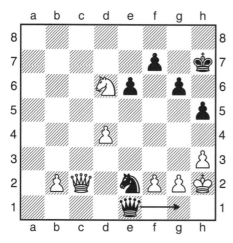

Khantuev – Ivenin
Irkutsk Ch 2010

Although it is White's move, and he is a pawn ahead, he resigned because he is helpless to prevent Black from winning. This is because Black has set up a tremendously strong mating pattern – featuring *a knight on the e2-square*, and *a queen on the opponent's back rank*. The threat is **1...♕g1 checkmate**. The move 1 h4 merely postpones matters: 1...♕g1+ 2 ♔h3 ♕h1 mate. In fact, White's only option to stop a quick mate is to give up queen for knight, a certain loss in the long run.

OK, perhaps in a game you could calculate hard and find this pattern by yourself, without knowing it beforehand. But how far in advance could you correctly assess this next 'Mighty Mate' position, in which White has serious counterplay of his own?

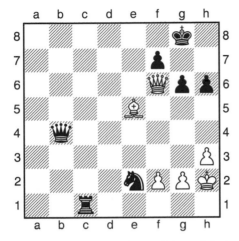

Black to move

J. Hartung – A. Pakhomov

Pardubice 2006

If Black were inexperienced, he might be very worried by White's threat of ♕g7 checkmate. However, for a player familiar with pattern recognition, the tempo-winning solution is routine: **1...♖h1+!** and White resigned, seeing **2 ♔xh1 ♕e1+** (2...♕b1+ also sets up the 'Mighty Mate' formation) **3 ♔h2 ♕g1 checkmate**.

A master-level player would spot the winning rook-sacrifice combination *in a couple of seconds*, as the theme is well-known.

THE ROOK-LIFT

Not all tactical finishes are quite so standard. The setting in the diagram below fooled White, a master-strength player. At this point, it is not immediately obvious how our checkmate pattern is going to arise.

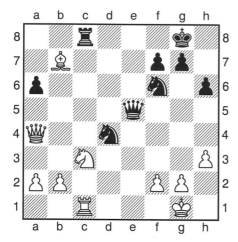

Black to move
W. Koch – Buhmann
Germany (teams) 2004/5

1...♖xc3! 2 ♖xc3 ♕e1+ 3 ♔h2 ♘e2 White resigns. Although White can give a few checks (4 ♖c8+ ♔h7 5 ♗e4+ g6), he is powerless against the mating formation. Black, the winner of this game, is a grandmaster – the highest title you can have in chess, apart from World Champion.

Some tips for solving the **100 Chess Puzzles**.
- The introduction to each puzzle usually explains the pattern from **White's point of view**. So if there is a puzzle with Black to move, you'll need to transpose the concept in your mind; e.g., *a white queen sacrifice on h7* would become a *black queen sacrifice on h2*. It may seem a bit complex at first, but it is all part of learning about chess – and with practice it becomes easy.
- Each puzzle page contains two diagrams. Puzzle A (with helpful arrows) teaches an important concept. Puzzle B is the tough one for solving – can you find the right continuation in a similar (but not identical) position? If you like, cover the solution in Puzzle B with a small piece of card, to avoid seeing it by accident.
- Finally, do remember that in chess books, we don't always analyse hopeless defensive attempts. Perhaps instead of following a critical main line, you see that the defender can avoid mate by giving up a piece. Well done for spotting this – but it does not mean the puzzle is flawed! We take it for granted that if a combination wins major material, it has been successful.

In our final illustrative position, two grandmasters are playing each other. Remarkably, Black has two queens, yet the deadly 'Mighty Mate' formation decides the game in White's favour.

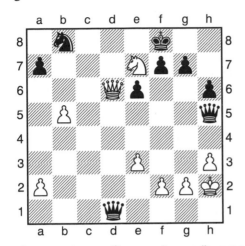

White to move
Bacrot – Svetushkin
French League 2012

1 ♘g6++ ♚g8 2 ♕xb8+ ♚h7 3 ♘e7 Black resigns. Beautiful play by White – even with an extra queen, Black has no acceptable defence to the threat of 4 ♕g8 checkmate.

As we can see, there are *many different ways a single theme can be used* – and knowing the most standard concepts will give you a huge head-start. Had you seen all of the above versions before? If not, for sure you will absorb these concepts for the future – and so you are already a slightly stronger player. I guarantee that the cumulative effect of knowing a few hundred such patterns will make you a very dangerous opponent indeed!

1 PICKING OFF THE PIECES

Lining up a queen & bishop to threaten checkmate is a standard attacking procedure. Usually the aim is a kingside attack – but occasionally a stray piece on the queenside is there for the taking.

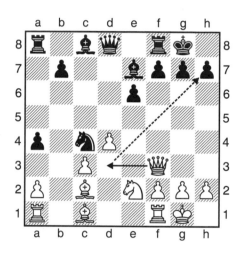

1a) White moves

Kernazhitsky-A.Yanovsky, Kiev Ch 2007

The black knight on c4 is unprotected. White can win it with a *fork* – a double attack.

1 ♕d3 Black resigns. The white queen has lined up in front of the bishop to threaten ♕xh7 mate. Black can stop checkmate – but loses the knight; e.g., 1...g6 2 ♕xc4.

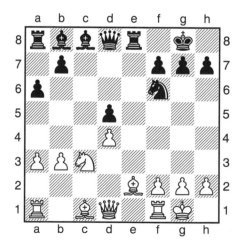

1b) Black moves

Nadir-Magerramov, Abu Dhabi 2003

The white knight on the c3-square is unprotected. Can you find Black's winning fork?

1...♕c7 White resigns. A knight will be lost – so White gives up. After 2 g3 (in order to stop 2...♕xh2 checkmate) comes 2...♕xc3.

THE CLASSIC FORK WITH ♕e4

2

Inexperienced players often lose a rook to this trap. The white queen moves to e4 – threatening checkmate *and* a black rook. It is a fork – a double attack – and Black cannot deal with both threats at once.

2a) White moves

Wainwright-A.Robinson
England-USA Cable Match 1907

Players have been mislaying rooks to this fork for over 100 years.

1 ♕e4 White threatens 2 ♕h7 mate, and also 2 ♕xa8 – a great fork! **1...♖d8 2 ♕xa8** White wins. Black stopped the checkmate, but did not have time to save his rook.

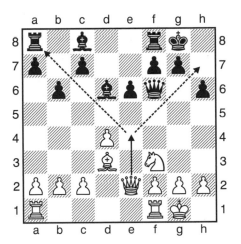

2b) White moves

Standard Opening Trap

This trap is common in amateur games. To set up a winning fork, White first has to remove a black defender. Can you see how to do this?

1 ♗xf6 (a clever swap – the black knight was defending both e4 and h7) **1...♗xf6 2 ♕e4** and White wins.

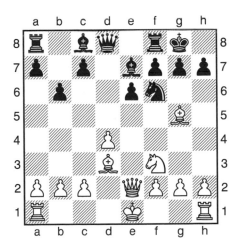

3 THE TWO-MOVE KNOCKOUT

A lethal two-move combination. First the white queen takes up an active position, threatening mate. Black defends with a pawn move – only to have his kingside obliterated with a knock-out sacrifice.

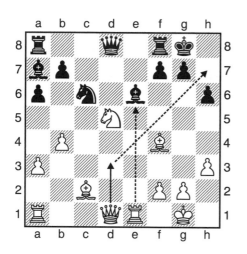

3a) White moves

Cuenca Jimenez-Cabrera Galeano
Albacete 2005

White starts by threatening ♕h7 mate. Then a rook sacrifice smashes Black's position apart.

1 ♕d3 g6 2 ♖xe6! Black resigns. After 2...fxe6 – or else Black is a bishop down – comes 3 ♕xg6+ ♔h8 4 ♕h7 checkmate.

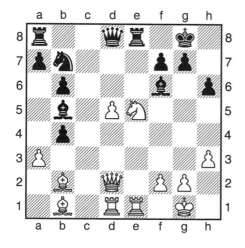

3b) White moves

S.Ernst-R.Odendahl, Dieren 2004

White won in two moves by threatening a decisive queen penetration.

1 ♕c2 g6 (or else 2 ♕h7+ is crushing) **2 ♘xf7! Black resigns**. On 2...♔xf7, 3 ♕xg6+ is decisive. Bad luck if you chose the less forcing 2 ♘xg6?, as 2...♗xb2 defends.

THE MEGA-KNOCKOUT

Your opponents won't know what's hit them when you play this double piece sacrifice combination. Once again, the black king is under pressure from the white queen & bishop line-up.

4a) White moves

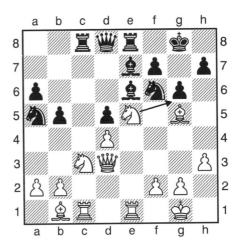

Smerdon-Cunanan, Canberra 2007

White gives up a knight but gets back a pawn and bishop – a great trade.

1 ♘xg6! hxg6 2 ♖xe6! This combination wins a pawn, because Black dare not capture the rook. On 2...fxe6 White checkmates with 3 ♕xg6+ ♔h8 (or 3...♔f8 4 ♗h6 mate) 4 ♗xf6+ ♗xf6 5 ♕h7 mate.

4b) White moves

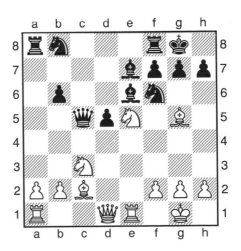

E.Hossain-Mehar, Bhubaneswar 2011

The full-length knockout is a three-move sequence. How does White win a pawn by force?

1 ♕d3 (threatening 2 ♗xf6 and 3 ♕xh7 mate) **1...g6 2 ♘xg6! hxg6 3 ♖xe6!**.

5 MORE QUEEN & BISHOP LINE-UPS

There are many combinations possible where the white queen and bishop are lined up on the b1-h7 diagonal. To avoid being check-mated, Black often has to weaken his kingside pawn-structure.

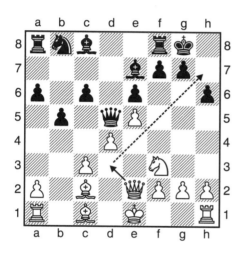

5a) White moves

Ftačnik-J.Zimmermann, Hamburg 2004

This pattern nets the h6-pawn. First White threatens the usual checkmate.

1 ♛d3 g6 Black has no good defence. 1...♖d8 2 ♛h7+ ♚f8 3 ♛h8 is still mate, and 1...f5 lets the white queen penetrate: 2 exf6 ♝xf6 3 ♛h7+. **2 ♝xh6** White has won a pawn.

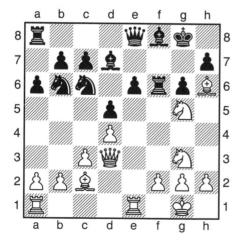

5b) White moves

Rodi-Macedo, Natal 2011

White has weakened Black's kingside by using the queen & bishop line-up. What unusual idea now wins material?

1 ♞h5! ♖f5 (1...gxh5 2 ♛xh7 mate) **2 ♛xf5! Black resigns**. A neat fork will win rook for knight: 2...gxf5 3 ♞f6+ ♚h8 4 ♞xe8.

16

THE ♘g6 TRICK

This trap is seen frequently. The defender mistakenly assumes the g6-square is out of bounds to the white knight.

6a) White moves

Standard Opening Trap

This white knight fork is common in lower-level events. Black simply misses the threat.

1 ♘g6! A disaster for Black – the queen and rook are forked. White's knight cannot be captured as the black f7-pawn is pinned (against the king) by the white bishop on b3.

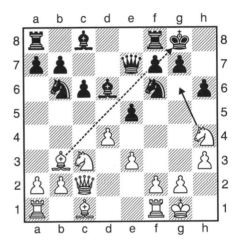

6b) Black moves

Kreischer-Nickl, Gmunden 2005

A normal-looking position – yet after Black's next move, White resigned. What was the winning move, and why was it so strong?

1...♘g3! White resigns. His queen is trapped!

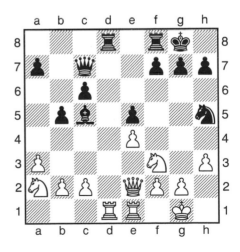

7 THE ♗xh6/♕g6+ COMBO

In this theme, White's dark-squared bishop is sacrificed on h6, ruining Black's defensive pawn-structure. Then the waiting white queen penetrates to the g6-square – giving check and starting a huge attack.

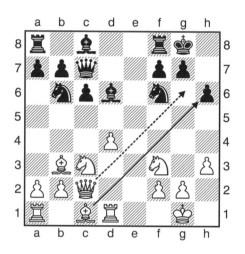

7a) White moves

Ma.Mader-S.Häcker
German Women's League 2011/12

Note that the white bishop on b3 pins Black's f7-pawn – essential for this idea to work.

1 ♗xh6! gxh6 2 ♕g6+ The intruding queen cannot be captured. **2...♔h8 3 ♕xf6+** White has won back her piece with an extra pawn and an attack.

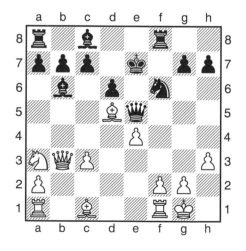

7b) Black moves

Jobava-Aronian, European Ch, Antalya 2004

White had opened with a swashbuckling Evans Gambit. How did Aronian now turn the tables – and show it is Black who is really attacking?

1...♗xh3! wins a pawn and weakens the white kingside. If 2 gxh3 ♕g3+ 3 ♔h1 ♕xh3+ 4 ♔g1 ♘g4, mate is coming.

THE ♞f6+/♛g6+ COMBO

Do you see the similarities with the previous puzzle? This time you get to sacrifice your knight to rupture the black pawn-structure. And please remember – *a white bishop is needed on the a2-g8 diagonal.*

8a) White moves

Dolzhikova-Al.Zakharova
Evpatoria (Under-18 Girls) 2005

White attacks the black king with a long and forcing series of moves.

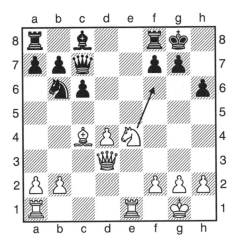

1 ♞f6+! gxf6 If 1...♚h8, 2 ♛h7 mate. **2 ♛g6+ ♚h8 3 ♛xh6+ ♚g8 4 ♛g6+ ♚h8 5 ♛xf6+ ♚g8 6 ♛g5+ ♚h8 7 ♜e4 Black resigns**. The white rook boosts the attack: mate by 8 ♜h4 is threatened.

8b) Black moves

Staniszewski-Av.Grigorian, Warsaw 2008

A tough puzzle. A knight on e2 helps the defence – but there is still a win for Black, seven moves deep.

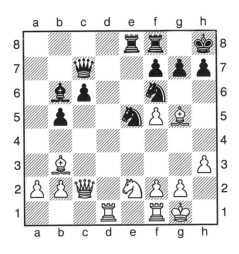

1...♞f3+! 2 gxf3 ♜xe2! (removing the piece that defends g3) **3 ♛xe2 ♛g3+ 4 ♚h1 ♛xh3+ 5 ♚g1 ♝c7! 6 f4 ♞g4 White resigns**. 7 f3 ♝b6+ is decisive.

19

HOW TO BEAT A WORLD CHAMPION

Russian superstar Vladimir Kramnik once fell for this trick.
The ♕g6 check is easy to miss – at first glance
it appears this square is protected by Black's f7-pawn.

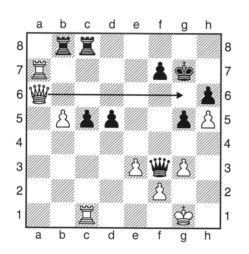

9a) White moves

Ponomariov-Kramnik, Wijk aan Zee 2003

The white rook on a7 is *pinning* the black f7-pawn. This allows a surprise queen check.

1 ♕g6+ Black resigns. The black kingside pawns fall off after 1...♔f8 (or 1...♔h8) 2 ♕xh6+ followed by 3 ♕xg5+.

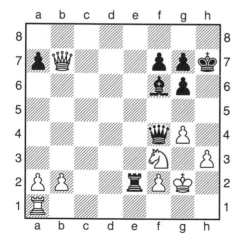

9b) Black moves

Zl.Stojanović-Weinzetti, Senta 2008

1...♖xb2 2 ♕xa7 is at best unclear. Instead, from the diagram position, can you spot *two* creative ideas to trouble the white king?

1...♗h4! 2 ♖f1 ♕g3+ 3 ♔h1 ♕xh3+ favoured Black in the game. Idea two: 1...♗e5 (to play 2...♕g3+) 2 ♔f1 ♖xb2.

CENTRAL COLLAPSE

Be alert to this crushing knight sacrifice possibility if the black f7-pawn moves early in the game. Although brief, this combination features three tactical motifs: *removing the defender*, *decoy* and *pin*.

10a) White moves

Al Modiahki-Al Sayad
Arab Ch, Casablanca 2002

Last move Black unwisely advanced his f7-pawn.

1 ♘xe6! This capture wipes out the black pawn-centre. If Black takes the knight with **1...♕xe6, 2 ♗xd5** pins – and wins – the black queen. The game ended **1...♖fe8 2 ♘c5 Black resigns**.

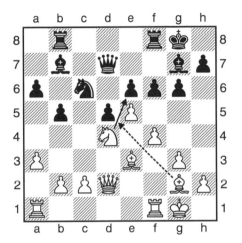

10b) White moves

Goriachkina-Severina, Kharkov (women) 2012

Here the top-rated 14-year-old girl in Europe shows her tactical flair. Can you find the win too?

1 ♗xf6! (removing a key defender of d5) **1...♗xf6 2 ♘xe6 Black resigns**. If **2...♕xe6 3 ♗xd5** the queen is lost, and otherwise the black position is a wreck.

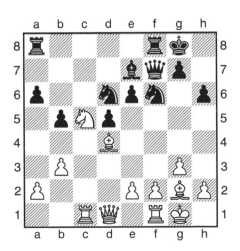

21

THE ♘xe6/♖xe6 COMBO

When a white rook, white knight and white bishop are all aimed at the black e6-pawn, the position is screaming out for a knight sacrifice.

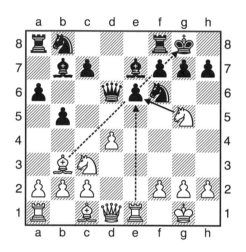

11a) White moves

Khachiyan-I.Serpik
Southern California Ch, Costa Mesa 2003

The grandmaster playing White will have spotted this pattern in seconds.

1 ♘xe6! wins. If 1...fxe6, 2 ♖xe6 threatens the black queen, *and a deadly discovered check* (e.g., 2...♕d8 3 ♖d6+). The game ended **1...♖e8 2 ♗f4 Black resigns**.

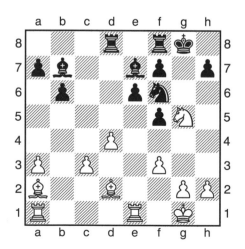

11b) White moves

Jo.Nun-B.Balogh, Warsaw 1978

With queens swapped off, could a sacrifice really still work? You decide.

1 ♘xe6! fxe6 2 ♖xe6 (amazing – the threat of discovered check is so strong that White will regain his piece) **2...♗d5** (or 2...♔f7 3 ♖ae1! ♗xa3 4 ♖e7++) **3 ♖xe7** and White is two pawns up.

22

A BACKWARD PAWN ON e6

A *backward pawn* is a weakness to target as it is fixed in position, and undefended by other pawns. When a black e6-pawn becomes backward, the attack down the semi-open file can be very sudden.

12a) White moves

R.Zentgraf-Huhnstock
Germany Under-25 Ch, Oberhof 2010

The e6-pawn is *backward* – and is also *on the same diagonal as the black king*.

1 ♖xe6! Black resigns. The rook sacrifice opens the diagonal and removes a defender of the knight on d5. If 1...♕xe6 2 ♗xd5 the white bishop pins and wins the black queen.

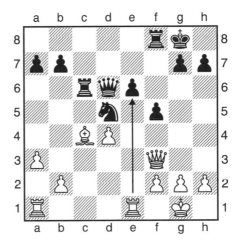

12b) White moves

Steingrimsson-Fl.Perez, Reykjavik 2012

This motif of this opening trap is worth noting. How can White win the e6-pawn – and more?

1 c5! (opening the a2-g8 diagonal for the c2-bishop) **1...bxc5 2 ♖xe6! ♕xe6** (2...♕d8 3 ♖xd6) **3 ♗b3** and Black gets insufficient compensation for his queen.

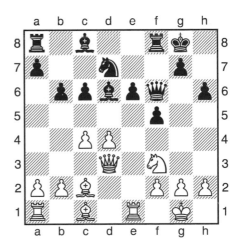

23

13 KNIGHTMARE ON e6

There are many fine combinations where White sacrifices a knight on the e6-square. In this frequently-seen version, the usual *white bishop on the a2-g8 diagonal* provides support.

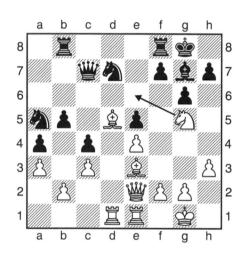

13a) White moves

Van Kampen-S.Kuipers, Wijk aan Zee 2010

Here the knight move forks queen and rook – so Black has little choice but to capture.

1 ♘e6! fxe6 2 ♗xe6+ ♔h8 3 ♗xd7 The neat combination has won a pawn, and after **3...♛c6 4 ♕g4** White dominates the board as well.

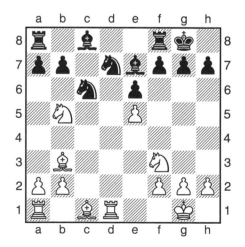

13b) White moves

A.Simonović-B.Vujačić
Serbian Team Ch, Vrnjačka Banja 2005

How did White, an international master, win a pawn from this position?

1 ♘c7 ♖b8 2 ♘xe6! wins at least a pawn. If **2...fxe6 3 ♗xe6+ ♔h8 4 ♗xd7 ♖d8**, White has 5 e6 with a winning position.

MORE KNIGHTMARES ON e6

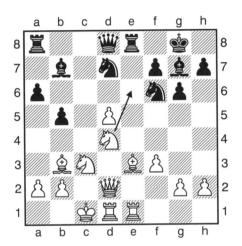

World Champion Garry Kasparov once used this idea to beat Nigel Short in just 33 moves. After sacrificing his knight, White aims to recapture on the e6-square with a pawn.

14a) White moves

Istratescu-Gallagher, Swiss Team Ch 2010

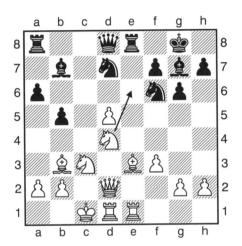

Note that after the white pawn recaptures on e6, a deadly *discovered check* is threatened.

1 ♘e6! fxe6 2 dxe6 ♔h8 2...♘b6 3 e7+ would cost Black his queen. **3 exd7 ♖e7** White is better. **4 ♗g5 ♖xd7 5 ♕xd7! ♕xd7 6 ♖xd7 ♘xd7 7 ♖e7** with a winning endgame.

14b) White moves

Epishin-del Rio Angelis, Albacete 2004

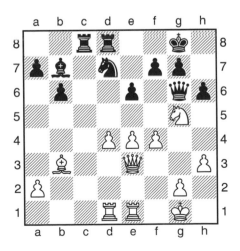

A creative version from GM Epishin. Can you spot the amazing concept?

1 ♘xe6! The point is 1...fxe6 2 f5! **♕f6** 3 fxe6, threatening two discovered checks. The end was **1...♖e8 2 f5 ♕f6 3 ♖f1! ♕e7 4 e5 Black resigns**. 4...fxe6 5 fxe6 with 6 ♖f7 to follow.

THE KILLER
♕f3/♘f5 SET-UP (1)

This aggressive formation will win you games for sure. A *white queen on f3* cooperates beautifully in attack with a *white knight on f5*.

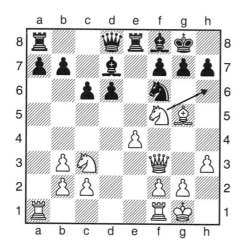

15a) White moves

Degremont-E.Gilles, Aix-les-Bains 2003

This motif has claimed many victims over the years.

1 ♘h6+! gxh6 The trouble for Black is that 1...♔h8 loses to 2 ♘xf7+, a knight fork of king and queen. **2 ♗xf6 ♗e7 3 ♕g3+ Black resigns.** Mate is imminent with ♕g7.

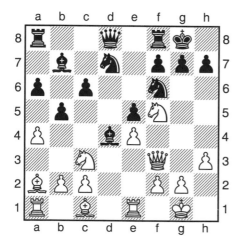

15b) White moves

Bojkov-Fa.Molina, Bergamo 2009

Here a different attacking manoeuvre wins material. What did White play?

1 ♗h6! The bishop cannot be captured, due to 1...gxh6 2 ♕g3+. Also 1...♘e8 2 ♕g3 ♕f6 fails to 3 ♗g5 ♕g6 4 ♘e7+. So Black chose **1...g6**, which loses rook for bishop.

THE KILLER ♛f3/♞f5 SET-UP (2)

16

A *queen on f3* and a *knight on f5* are often supported by White's dark-squared bishop. If Black has a pawn on the h6-square, he had better watch out. White bishop sacrifices are constantly in the air.

16a) White moves

Goganov-Duzhakov, Peterhof 2010

White's pieces are beautifully placed, and the black pawn on h6 is a tempting target...

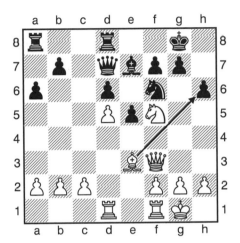

1 ♗xh6! This move wins a pawn, because if 1...gxh6 White has the typical queen-check follow-up 2 ♕g3+. For example, 2...♚f8 3 ♕g7+ ♚e8 4 ♕h8+ ♗f8 5 ♕xf6.

16b) Black moves

H.Kaplan-Fogarasi, Germany (teams) 2010/11

You'll need to foresee a neat finesse, or else White can defend...

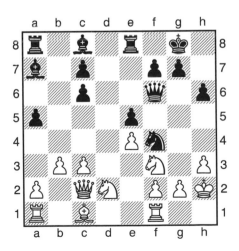

1...♗xh3! 2 gxh3 (White plans 2...♕g6? 3 ♞h4 ♕h5? 4 ♞df3, defending) **2...♕e6! White resigns**. After this sidestep (threatening 3...♕xh3+), 3 ♞g1 ♕g6 sets up an unstoppable mate on g2.

17 THE TRICKY ♕g3/♘g4 SET-UP

This piece formation makes some sneaky tactics possible, as the *white queen on g3 pins the g7-pawn*. This gives the white knight on g4 options of a handy check on the h6-square or (less often) the f6-square.

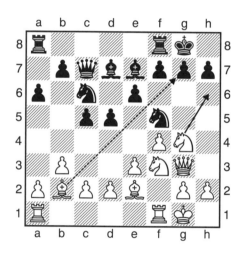

17a) White moves

Mavilis-H.Göring, Regensburg 1889

An old favourite. The black knight on f5 defends the g7-square, and attacks the white queen. But suddenly it all unravels...

1 ♘h6+! Black resigns. If 1...♘xh6, 2 ♕xg7 is mate. 1...♔h8 2 ♘xf5 is scarcely preferable as White has three pieces attacking g7.

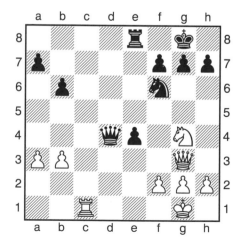

17b) White moves

E.Danielian-Chiburdanidze
Jermuk (women) 2010

Your chance to beat a famous Women's World Champion! What knight relocation has Black overlooked?

1 ♘h6+ Black resigns. Too late she sees the idea: 1...♔f8 2 ♘f5, threatening both ♕xg7 mate and the black queen.

THE QUIET KILLER: ♗f6

This attacking concept arises often, and can be crushingly strong. A modest bishop move to the f6-square gums up the black defence – and corners the black king.

18a) White moves

Rendle-Luaces Rubio, Hastings 2011/12

White's rook wants to join the kingside attack. But on the immediate 1 ♖h4, Black defends with the freeing advance 1...f6 or 1...f5.

1 ♗f6! Black resigns. The bishop move stifles any hope of defence. 2 ♖h4 is a threat, and if 1...gxf6, then 2 ♖h4 anyway, with mate to follow.

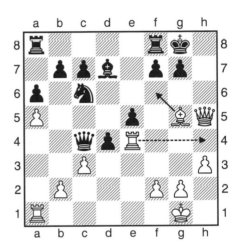

18b) White moves

Lenderman-Zierk, Las Vegas 2012

This super-tough challenge requires you to find five accurate moves in a row.

1 ♗f6! gxf6 2 ♖e3! e5 3 ♕h6 ♔h8 4 dxe5 ♕d8 5 ♖d3! (the only win) **Black resigns**. If 5...♕xd3, 6 ♕xf8 mate, or 5...♕e8 6 ♕xf6+ ♔g8 7 ♖g3+ and mate next move, or 5...♗d7 6 ♖ad1, winning.

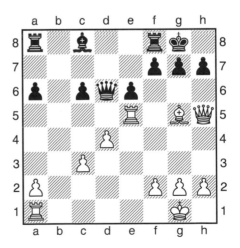

KNIGHT SACRIFICE ON f6

There are many variants of this classic, where the knight is sacrificed to *damage the pawn-structure around the enemy king*. With the black king's defensive protection shattered, enter the white queen stage left.

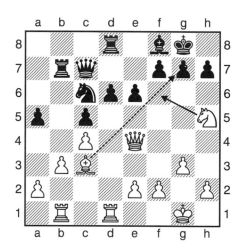

19a) White moves

Brøndum-W.Rosen
World Seniors Ch, Bad Zwischenahn 2008

Here the queen gets attacking support from a bishop on the a1-h8 diagonal.

1 ♘f6+! gxf6 Declining is not an option – 1...♔h8 2 ♕xh7 mate. **2 ♕g4+ Black resigns**. If 2...♔h8, 3 ♗xf6+ will mate, or 2...♗g7 3 ♗xf6 ♔f8 4 ♕xg7+ and White wins material.

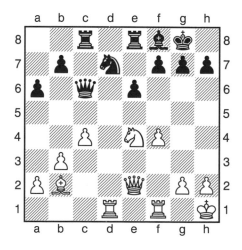

19b) White moves

Godula-L.Bojda, Slovakian Team Ch 2004/5

The knight on d7 is doing an important defensive job. Can you see why – and then work out White's winning move?

1 ♖xd7! ♕xd7 2 ♘f6+! gxf6 3 ♕g4+ Black resigns. After 3...♗g7 4 ♗xf6 Black cannot avoid checkmate next move with 5 ♕xg7.

MORE ♘f6+ SACRIFICES

As in the previous puzzle, a white knight sacrifice aims to expose the enemy king. And this time – though there are fewer pieces on the board – the heavy artillery is waiting.

20a) White moves

Shivaji-Thornally, San Francisco 2004

White's queen and rook are well placed to enter the attack.

1 ♘f6+! gxf6 2 ♕h6! Well played. Not 2 ♖g3+? ♔h8 3 ♕h6, when 3...♕xd4+ 4 ♔h1 ♖g8 defends. **2...♕xd4+ 3 ♔h1** and White wins, as 4 ♖g3+ is coming next move.

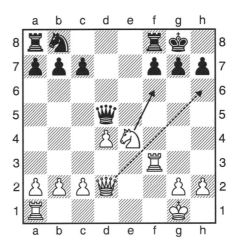

20b) White moves

Chatalbashev-Z.J.Szabo, Balatonlelle 2003

Last move Black refused the knight sacrifice, and moved his king instead. So what now?

1 ♖h3! (if 1 ♕h4?, 1...h6 defends) **Black resigns**. 1...♖xd4 2 ♖xh7 is mate, 1...h6 2 ♕f4 tees up for 3 ♖xh6+, and 1...gxf6 2 ♕xf6+ ♔g8 3 ♖g3 is mate.

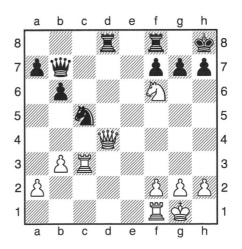

31

21 OPEN THE h-FILE WITH ♗g5

This useful attacking idea can occur when White has a *pawn on h4* and Black has a *pawn on h6*. White plays the shock move ♗g5. The bishop can be taken – but this opens the h-file leading to Black's king.

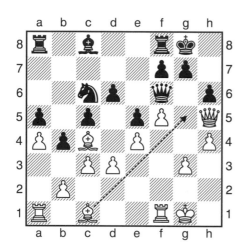

21a) White moves

I.Badjarani-K.Faisal, Abu Dhabi 2000

This h-file is forced open and White wins instantly.

1 ♗g5! hxg5 2 hxg5 Black resigns. 2...♕d8 3 g6 gives White a crushing attack. He threatens immediate checkmate with ♕h7.

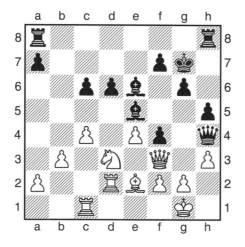

21b) Black moves

Nadi-Fe.Heinrich, Hungarian League 2008/9

Here White has extra firepower defending the g4-square. So what should Black play?

1...♗g4! wins regardless. It doesn't matter that White has 2 hxg4 hxg4 3 ♕xg4. Black makes use of the newly-opened h-file and plays 3...♕h1 mate.

FRIGHT KNIGHT 22

This fiendish knight jump transforms an ordinary position into a horror story for the defender. It occurs where a bishop and queen are both focused on the enemy g7-square (the g2-square if Black is attacking).

22a) Black moves

K.Mathe-Chirila
Romanian Junior Team Ch, Mangalia 2007

An amazing knight leap clears the path for the bishop to attack on the diagonal.

1...♞d2! 2 ♕xd2 If 2 ♞xd2, then 2...♕xg2 mate. **2...♝xf3 3 g3 ♕h5 4 ♖fe1 ♖f6 5 ♝f1 ♖h6 White resigns.** Maybe White saw only 6 h3? ♕xh3, as 6 h4 g5 7 ♝e2 restricts losses to a pawn.

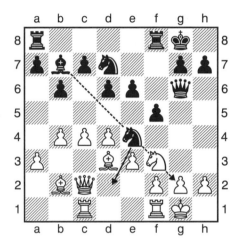

22b) White moves

Grek-Riitinki, Finnish Team Ch 2003/4

This time nail that coffin firmly shut. If you foresee White's crushing *fourth* move in the combination, you have a good eye for tactics.

1 ♞d7! ♖xd7 (the defence 1...♞h5 fails to 2 ♞f6+! ♞xf6 3 ♝xf6) **2 ♝xf6 g6 3 ♖xd7 ♕xd7 4 ♝xg6! Black resigns.**

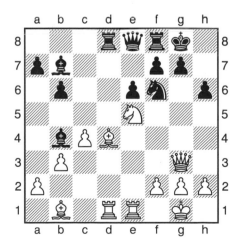

33

23 THE BELATED KING-HUNT

This king-hunt is most likely to occur in the late middlegame. First a
bishop is spectacularly sacrificed to draw out the enemy king.
Then a clever queen check cuts off any chance of retreat.

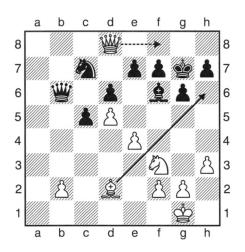

23a) White moves

Gongora Reyes-Adel Lahchaichi
Havana 2011

White's bold bishop sacrifice forces the
black king to leave its usual shelter.

1 ♗h6+! ♚xh6 2 ♕f8+ The key point –
there is no way back for the black king,
exposed on its third rank. **2...♗g7 3
♕xf7 g5 4 ♘h2 Black resigns**. The
threat is 5 ♘g4 mate.

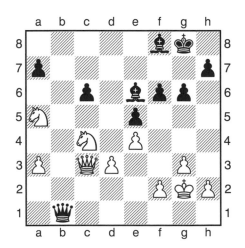

23b) Black moves

R.Granat-Bentley, British League 2004/5

How would you chase the white king
into enemy territory?

1...♗h3+! 2 ♚xh3 ♕f1+ 3 ♚g4 ♕g2!
(instructive: denied the f3 escape-square,
White's king is stranded) **4 h3 h5+ 5
♚h4 g5+ 6 ♚xh5 ♕xh3+ 7 ♚g6 ♗e7
White resigns**. 8...♕h7 mate follows.

TACTICS ON THE QUEENSIDE

Some less well-known themes are likely to occur on the queenside. This is because the black king is often on the c8-square – slightly closer to the centre than after kingside castling.

24a) White moves

Vallejo Pons-Maiwald
German League 2011/12

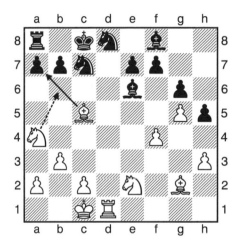

Here the black king has trekked to c8 on foot, but a bishop sacrifice catches him regardless.

1 ♗xa7! Black resigns. The threat is ♘b6 mate. Taking the bishop is no help: 1...♖xa7 2 ♘b6+ ♔b8 3 ♖xd8+ ♗c8 4 ♖xc8 mate.

24b) White moves

Vachier-Lagrave – Landenbergue
French League 2009

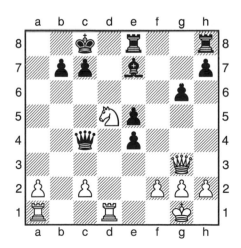

If 1 ♕xe5, then 1...♗d8 defends. So what move causes Black to resign?

1 ♘xe7+ Black resigns. It seems odd to swap the strong knight, until you see a flaw in Black's king position: 1...♖xe7 2 ♕a3! threatens 3 ♕xe7 and 3 ♕a8 mate.

25

FINISHING OFF
WITH ♖g4+

This theme occurs where the enemy king is slightly exposed.
The defender might think everything is holding – until a rook
sacrifice on the g4-square shatters both illusions and position.

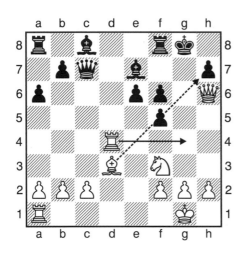

25a) White moves

Rooze-P.C.Wood
European Seniors Team Ch, Velden 2009

The white rook would love to move to
g4. But isn't the black f5-pawn cover-
ing this square?

1 ♖g4+! It turns out the rook check is
possible: 1...fxg4 2 ♕xh7 is mate thanks
to the bishop on d3. Other lines: 1...♔f7
2 ♕h5 mate and 1...♔h8 2 ♕g7 mate.

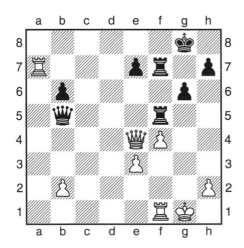

25b) Black moves

Art.Kovacs-Z.Erdelyi, Balatonlelle 2009

What move would you love to play?

1...♖g5+! White resigns. This neat tactic exploits the insufficiently protected
f1-rook – 2 fxg5 ♕xf1 is mate. The only
try is to grovel on with 2 ♔f2 ♕xb2+ 3
♔e1, a pawn down with a worse position.

THE SIMPLE ♗xg7 CAPTURE

When White has a bishop on the long diagonal, there are many versions of the ♗xg7 sacrifice. Perhaps the most basic is where White has a queen on the g-file, and a pawn on f5 or h5.

26a) White moves

Gyorgy-A.Mausz, Hungarian League 2007/8

The white bishop is temporarily given up, to be regained when the f-pawn advances.

1 ♗xg7! ♔xg7 2 f6 With this pawn advance, White regains the piece. The queen on g3 *pins* the black bishop. **2...♔f8 3 ♕xg7+** Black has avoided mate, but his position is a mess.

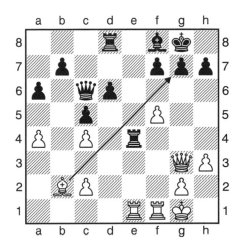

26b) White moves

S.Chekhov-Kostrikina, Voronezh 2012

After a ♗xg7 sacrifice, Black thought she could defend by putting a rook on c7. What reply had she overlooked?

1 ♖c5 Black resigns. As the black rook is tied to the c7-square (1...♖xc5 2 ♕xg7 mate) White's move effectively forks the black queen and rook.

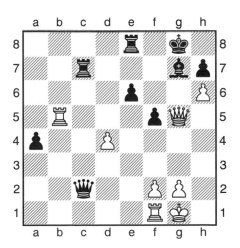

37

27 WINNING THE EXCHANGE

The chess term 'winning the exchange' means to win a rook (worth
five pawns) for a bishop or a knight (worth three pawns each).
Here is a formation that will win you rook for knight.

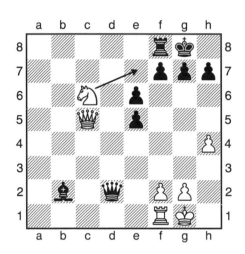

27a) White moves

Kramnik-Svidler
Monte Carlo (blindfold) 2004

This typical motif relies on the black
rook being defended only by its king.

1 ♘e7+ ♔h8 2 ♘g6+! White gives up
the knight – to get a rook in return.
2...hxg6 Forced – if 2...♔g8, 3 ♕xf8 is
mate! **3 ♕xf8+ ♔h7 4 ♕xf7** and White
later won.

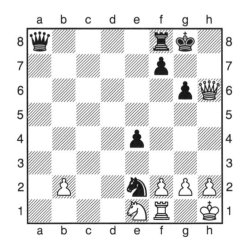

27b) Black moves

Pikula-Ivanisević
Montenegrin Team Ch, Cetinje 2009

Black is winning this pawn-down position. Can you spot the unusual idea?

1...♕a6! (creative – *an exchange* is won
by force, as the white rook is hemmed
in) **2 ♘c2 ♘g3+ 3 hxg3 ♕xf1+ 4 ♔h2
♕xf2 5 ♘e3 ♕xb2 White resigns**.

38

HUNGARIAN HORROR STORY

28a) Black moves

Zo.Varga-Boros, Budapest 2005

A Hungarian grandmaster is about to get a shock.

1...&a3! White resigns. The white b2-pawn – now attacked *by both knight and bishop* – is lost next move. The black bishop cannot be taken, since 2 bxa3 ♘xa3+ forks king and queen.

This pattern arises rarely – but is very nasty when it does. The defender's king and queen are on squares that allow a potential knight fork.

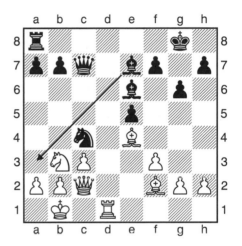

28b) White moves

Nevednichy-Pa.Petran
Hungarian League 2009/10

A fine move wins – but why doesn't the knight retreat ...♘e8 defend for Black?

1 &h6! ♘xf5 (if 1...♘e8, 2 &xg7! ♘xg7 3 ♘h6+ forks the king and queen anyway) **2 ♘xf5 g6 3 &xf8** and White has won the exchange, rook for bishop.

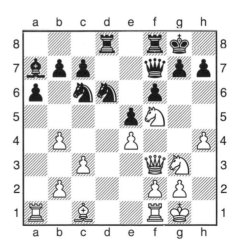

THE UNWELCOME VISITOR

If an attacking piece lands on the *g6-square*, it is usually bad news for the defender. Here the unwanted guest is a white bishop, working with a white knight on e5 to target the *f7-pawn*.

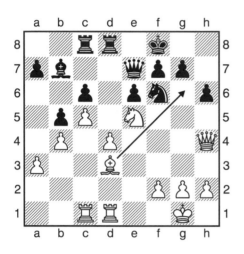

29a) White moves

Palau-Karlin, The Hague Olympiad 1928

This theme has been picking off f7-pawns for over 80 years.

1 ♗g6! A shock bishop move wins the f7-pawn for free. The motif works due to the positioning of the black king and queen – on 1...fxg6 comes the knight fork 2 ♘xg6+.

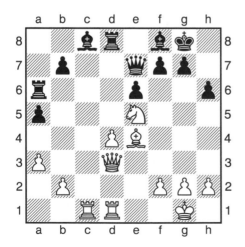

29b) White moves

Hulak-Rogić, Croatian Ch, Vukovar 2005

Here 1 ♗g6 would just lose a piece, as there is no knight fork. Can you make the idea work?

1 ♗h7+ (an instructive manoeuvre – Black's king is first forced to a forking square) **1...♔h8 2 ♗g6! f5 3 ♘f7+ ♔g8 4 ♘xd8** White has won rook for knight.

MORE ♗g6 BISHOP OFFERS

This bishop sacrifice (similar to the previous puzzle) is even harder for your opponent to foresee. The target is the *black f7-pawn*, and the offer is based on *the white queen being able to enter the attack.*

30a) White moves

W.Koch-Pilberg, Dortmund 1987

A sudden assault on the f7-pawn catches Black by surprise.

1 ♗g6! ♖f8 The white bishop cannot be taken: 1...fxg6 2 ♕xg6+ ♔f8 3 ♕f7 is checkmate. **2 ♗xf7** Anyway! White wins, because if 2...♖xf7, 3 ♕g6+ will mate next move.

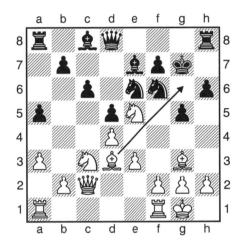

30b) White moves

Rasulov-V.Gaprindashvili, Esfahan 2011

This puzzle tests your creative abilities. What stunning move did White play?

1 ♗g6! Well done if you spotted this brilliant concept, putting the black f7-pawn under pressure. White's idea is 1...fxg6 2 ♕d3!; e.g., 2...♔f8 3 ♕xg6 and mate follows with ♕f7.

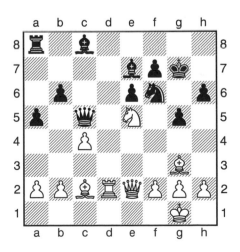

WINNING MATERIAL WITH ♘h6+

This terrific attacking set-up features *a white queen on g3* and *a white knight on f5*. Among other possibilities, you can often win pieces or pawns with *a knight check on the h6-square*.

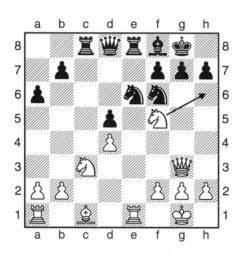

31a) White moves

D.Vinckier-Ann.Busch
French Women's League 2011

The classic trap. White wins the black queen with a knight fork – in just three moves.

1 ♘h6+ Black resigns. The knight can't be taken as the white queen *pins* the g7-pawn against the black king. 1...♔h8 allows 2 ♘xf7+ ♔g8 3 ♘xd8.

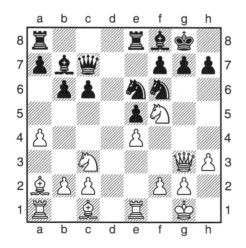

31b) White moves

Belikov-Kalegin, Alushta 2007

Here a Russian grandmaster cleverly wins a pawn. Can you work out how?

1 ♘h6+ ♔h8 2 ♕xe5! (very neat – if 2...♕xe5, then 3 ♘xf7+ ♔g8 4 ♘xe5, or worse 2...♗d6 3 ♕xd6!) **2...gxh6 3 ♕xf6+** and White is a pawn up with a great position.

THE ♗h6 EXCHANGE WIN 32

We have already learnt about the phrase 'winning the exchange' in Puzzle 27. In this standard theme, White wins a rook (worth five pawns) for a bishop (worth three pawns) – a profitable trade.

32a) White moves

A.Kovaliov-Dmitrenko, Alushta 2003

Moving the bishop to h6 is a standard exchange-winning motif.

1 ♗h6 g6 What else can Black do? Mate in one with ♕xg7 was threatened. **2 ♗xf8** White goes rook for bishop ahead, whichever way Black recaptures on f8.

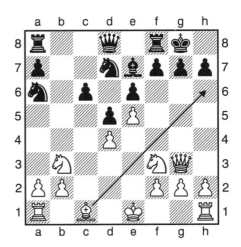

32b) White moves

W.Salamon-A.Jirovec
Austrian League 2007/8

A complex example. Can you see how to attack Black's 'Sicilian' formation?

1 f5! exf5 (if 1...dxe5, then 2 f6! ♗xf6 3 ♖xf6 or 1...♔h8 2 fxe6 dxe5 3 ♖xf7) **2 ♗h6 g6 3 ♗xf8** White's aggressive kingside play has won rook for bishop.

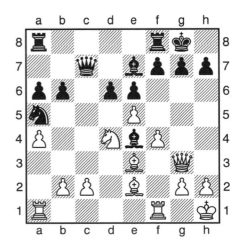

43

33 THE USEFUL ♞h5+ TRICK

This double-pin motif is a superb weapon to have in your arsenal of tricks. The pattern can arise in quite a number of different opening variations too.

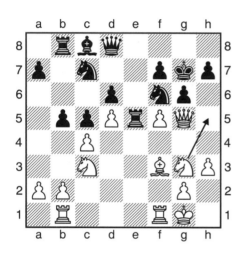

33a) White moves

Strenzke-W.Klotzki, Bargteheide 1989

Two points to note: the black queen is *undefended* and the black g6-pawn is *pinned*.

1 ♞h5+! Black resigns. White's check wins the black knight on f6, as the black king must retreat. Instead 1...♞xh5 loses the black queen to 2 ♕xd8.

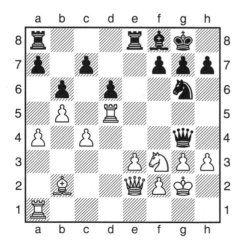

33b) Black moves

Man.Pohl-F.Mietner, Füssen 1993

White has just played 1 h3, threatening the black queen. Why was this a bad idea?

1...♞h4+! 2 ♔f1 (the white queen on e2 is undefended, meaning Black wins after 2 ♞xh4 ♕xe2) **2...♕xf3** Black wins a knight since 3 gxh4 ♕h1 is mate.

ANOTHER USEFUL ♘h5+ TRICK

34

In this theme the white queen is on the *e5-square* – where it *pins* the black knight. So after White plays ♘h5+, Black must capture with his pawn. This exposes the black king to a queen check on the g5-square.

34a) White moves

S.Darr-Womacka, Germany (teams) 2007/8

Black's knight is pinned against his king. This enables White to 'swap' knights in style.

1 ♘h5+! gxh5 2 ♕g5+ ♔f8 3 ♕xf6 White's smart little sequence has left Black's kingside pawns a wreck. Shortly White will capture the h5-pawn for free.

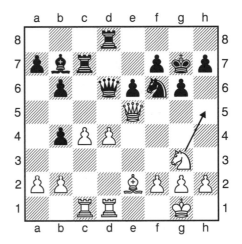

34b) White moves

Belikov-Lutsko, Voronezh 1997

How did White gain a huge attack – even with his rook on g5 threatened?

1 ♘f4! (1 ♘g3! is based on the same idea) **1...hxg5 2 ♘h5+! ♔h6** (2...gxh5 3 ♕xg5+ ♔h8 4 ♕xf6+ leads to a quick mate) **3 ♘xf6** Black is in big trouble; e.g., 3...♗c6 4 ♘g4+ ♔h7 5 ♕xg5!.

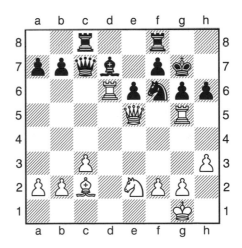

45

35 SURPRISE SKEWERS

If you see a chance to get your opponent's queen
and rook lined up on the same diagonal, it's time to
stop and think. Is a skewer possible?

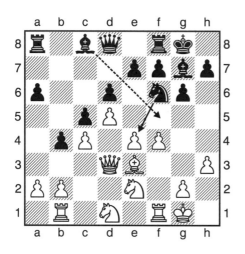

35a) Black moves

Hampek-Konigova, Plzen (Under-18) 1999

A shock move exploits a line-up of the white queen and rook on the b1-h7 diagonal.

1...♘xe4! This wins a pawn, because if White captures the knight with 2 ♕xe4, he gets hit by the *skewer* 2...♗f5. The queen can escape, but the rook is lost: 3 ♕f3 ♗xb1.

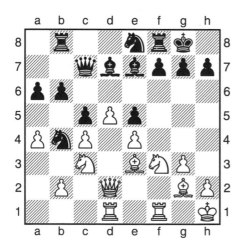

35b) White moves

Mir.Medić-Deur
Croatian Women's Ch, Topusko 2012

What surprise move – based on a skewer – did White play in this position?

1 ♘xe5! ♕xe5 (or else a central pawn is lost for nothing) **2 ♗f4** (skewering the queen and rook) **2...♕h5 3 ♗xb8** White is ahead on material, and should win.

In the positions below, Black is vulnerable in quite a subtle way: his queenside pawns are *all on light-coloured squares*. This causes weaknesses on his dark squares – which is sometimes a problem.

36a) White moves

Cappello-Passerotti, Rome 1979

A black structure with pawns on a6, b7 and c6 is sometimes OK. But in this position, the white pieces can exploit the weaknesses.

1 ♘b6 ♖b8 2 ♗c5+ ♔e8 3 ♗d6 Black resigns. The black rook is trapped, and the unstoppable threat is 4 ♗xb8.

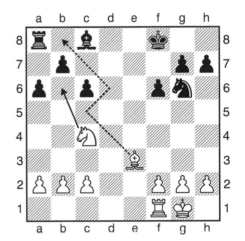

36b) White moves

Kalegin-Kutliarov, Ufa 2006

Can you find a graphic way to exploit Black's dark-squared weaknesses?

1 ♖xd8+! (this sacrifice eliminates the sole defender of Black's dark squares) **1...♔xd8 2 ♘b6 ♖a7 3 ♗b8** The trapped black rook will shortly be captured, leaving White a piece up.

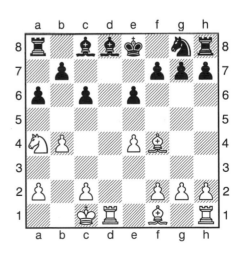

37 | A DELIGHTFUL DECOY

This super-advanced decoy pattern can create magnificent combinations. It features *a bishop decoy sacrifice* followed by *a knight fork*. It is so forcing it can sometimes win you a rook and a queen!

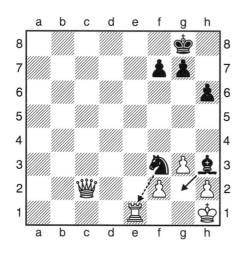

37a) Black moves

Basic pattern

Because the theme is so advanced, it is best to illustrate it initially with a made-up position.

1...♗g2+! This bishop decoy sacrifice forces the white king onto the g2-square. **2 ♔xg2 ♘xe1+** Now the black knight forks king and queen. **3 ♔f1 ♘xc2** Amazing – Black wins.

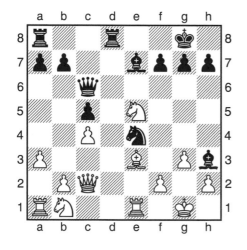

37b) Black moves

Rozentalis-B.Socko, Austrian League 2011/12

Decoys, forks, sacrifices... if you can't solve it, enjoy the spectacular solution.

1...♘d2! (threatening ...♕g2 mate) **2 ♘xc6 ♘f3+ 3 ♔h1 ♗g2+! 4 ♔xg2 ♘xe1+ 5 ♔h3 ♘xc2 6 ♘xe7+ ♔f8 7 ♗xc5 ♘xa1 8 ♘c6+ ♔e8 9 ♘xd8 ♔xd8** and Black is better. Wow!

48

A decoy sacrifice can be used to *win a tempo* – chess terminology for 'gaining time'. If the enemy king is forced onto a checking square, it can be like having a free move to pursue your attack.

38a) White moves

Spielmann-Bogoljubow
Match game 5, Semmering 1932

White's queen is threatened, so 1 ♘xe8? fails to 1...♘xf3+. Time for a decoy sacrifice.

1 ♗g7+! This decoy forces the black king *onto a checking square*. **1...♔xg7 2 ♘xe8+** Now the knight capture is with check. **2...♔h6 3 ♕xf7 Black resigns**.

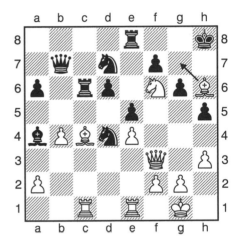

38b) White moves

Barlov-E.Rayncr, Groningen 1974/5

White's queen is attacked. How did he *gain time* to exploit a discovered check?

1 ♗g7+! ♔xg7 2 ♘e8++ (this *double check* is the point; 2 ♘h5++ is similar) **2...♔h6** (or 2...♔g8 3 ♕g7 mate) **3 ♕g7+ Black resigns**. 3...♔g5 4 h4+ ♔g4 5 ♗h3+ ♔h5 6 ♕xh7 checkmate.

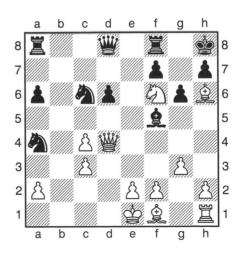

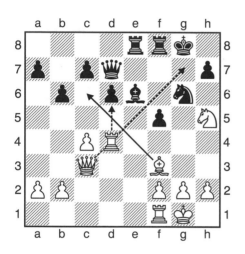

39 | DAZZLING DEFLECTIONS

A *deflection* occurs when a defending piece is forced away from a square where it carries out a vital duty. Are you ready to spot deep tactics over the whole board? These puzzles will stretch you.

39a) White moves

Malakhov-Salgado Lopez
European Ch, Plovdiv 2012

This deflection targets the black queen, currently on guard duty against ♕g7 mates.

1 ♗c6! Black resigns. The dramatic bishop skewer is based on the line 1...♕xc6 2 ♖xd6!, with the double threat of 3 ♖xc6 and 3 ♕g7 checkmate.

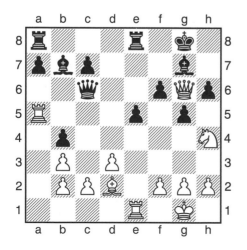

39b) White moves

Bojkov-Van Riemsdijk, Queenstown 2012

1 ♘f5 is a killer – except for 1...♕xg2 mate. Can you deflect Black's queen?

1 ♖c5! (White plays a brilliant rook sacrifice) **1...♕xc5 2 ♘f5 ♖e7** (or 2...♕f8 3 ♗xb4! c5 4 ♗xc5! ♕f7 5 ♘xh6+) **3 d4** and there is no good square for Black's attacked queen to move to.

50

This theme – *a bishop sacrifice* followed by *a knight fork* – shatters the enemy kingside at a stroke. You'll need to analyse three or more moves ahead to play a combination of this quality.

40a) Black moves

Haessel-U.Iyengar, Freemont 2012

Black could fork king and rook – if only the white bishop weren't guarding the e2-square.

1...♗xg2! White resigns. The point is 2 ♔xg2 ♘e2+ 3 ♔f1 ♘xc3, and Black wins. If White doesn't accept the bishop sacrifice, he is a pawn down with a smashed kingside.

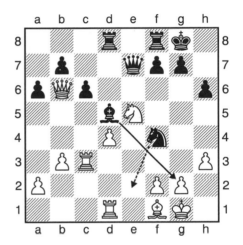

40b) Black moves

Vl.Gerber-Popovkin, Kiev Ch 2008

The white king and queen sit on squares vulnerable to a knight fork. But how to deal with *two* white pieces guarding the e2-square?

1...♖xd1 2 ♖xd1 (one defender of e2 gone) **2...♗xg2!** wins, because 3 ♔xg2 ♘e2+ forks king and queen.

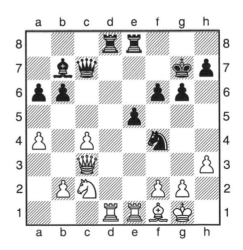

TAL'S TALLINN TRICK

This unexpected tactic can occur early in the opening – and often wins *an exchange* (rook for bishop). Our illustrative puzzle stars ex-World Champion Mikhail Tal, perhaps the greatest chess tactician of all.

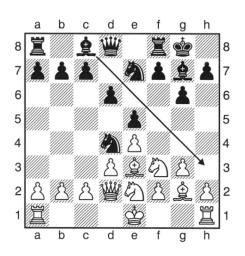

41a) Black moves

Barcza-Tal, Tallinn 1971

The Magician from Riga makes a bishop offer that White cannot accept...

1...♗h3! As 2 ♗xh3 ♘xf3+ is a knight fork of king and queen. Or 2 0-0 ♘xf3+ 3 ♗xf3 ♗xf1 and Black wins rook for bishop. **2 ♘fxd4 ♗xg2 3 ♖g1 exd4** and White was a piece for a pawn down.

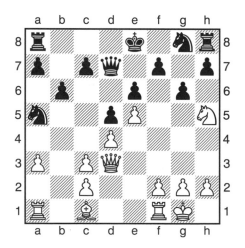

41b) White moves

Dworakowska-Morkisz, Polish League 2007

Yet imagine even Tal's version can be trumped. What fantastic idea wins for White?

1 ♗h6! A remarkable shot. If 1...gxh5, 2 ♗g7 traps the black rook, and the response to 1...♘xh6 is 2 ♘f6+, forking the black king and queen.

THE ♗a6 TRAP

42

This is more a classy deflection than a sacrifice, as White gets the piece back straightaway. The white bishop offers itself on the a6-square to *undermine the defence of the black knight on the c6-square*.

42a) White moves

Cori Tello-Nakhbaeva
World Girls' Ch, Chennai 2011

Is the action on the kingside or queen-side? The bishop offer is easy to miss.

1 ♗a6! Now if 1...♗xa6, White wins a piece with 2 ♘xc6 ♕d7 3 ♘xe7+. Black tried **1...♘xe5** but after **2 ♗xb7 ♘g6 3 ♗xa8 ♕xa8** White ended up rook for bishop ahead.

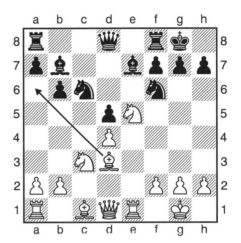

42b) White moves

Advanced Opening Trap

The move 1 ♗a6! has caught out many strong players. Your puzzle question: how does White win if Black plays 1...♗xa6 in reply?

1 ♗a6! ♗xa6 allows White a crushing finish with **2 ♘xc6 ♕c7 3 ♘xe7+ ♕xe7 4 ♗xf6**.

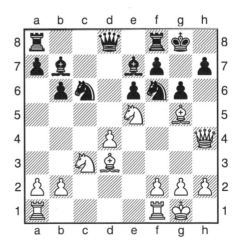

THE ROOK & KNIGHT DECOY

These standard decoy combinations are very forcing.
First a rook sacrifice lures the enemy queen to a target square.
Then a follow-up knight check forks king and queen.

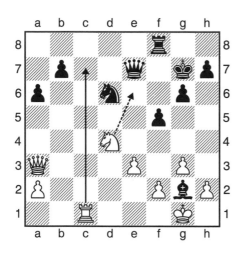

43a) White moves

Lazić-Bozanić, Split 2010

Instead of a routine bishop recapture (with 1 ♔xg2) White plays a *rook decoy sacrifice*.

1 ♖c7! The rook pins the queen, so Black must capture or lose his queen. **1...♕xc7 2 ♘e6+** The black queen is lost anyway, to a knight fork.

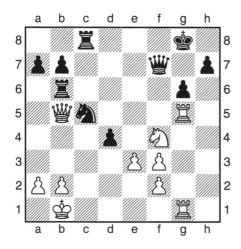

43b) White moves

Bogdanov-Karpachev, Bad Wiessee 2006

How well can you analyse a long sequence of captures, checks and forcing moves?

1 ♖xc5! ♖xb5 2 ♖xc8+ ♔g7 3 ♖c7! (regaining the queen) **3...♕xc7 4 ♘e6+ ♔f7 5 ♘xc7** and, a piece up, White wins. 5...♖c5 6 ♖c1 rescues the knight.

MASTERING THE ZWISCHENZUG

A *zwischenzug* is chess terminology meaning 'in-between move'.
In the middle of a sequence of seemingly obvious moves,
there comes an unexpected interpolation – often a check.

44a) White moves

Hort-F.Slingerland, Hoogeveen 2006

Black's attempt to swap rooks allows White to a win a rook, due to a *zwischenzug* on move two.

1 ♖xc4 Threatening 2 ♕xa7+, so a queen trade is forced. **1...♕xf2 2 ♖c7+!** **Black resigns**. By inserting the check, White saves his rook and wins; e.g., 2...♔f8 3 ♘xf2.

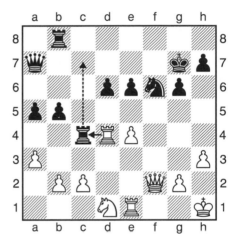

44b) White moves

Tikkanen-Sv.Pedersen, Borup 2010

Hidden in this position is a devious combination to win material. Can you find it?

1 ♗xe4 ♘xe4 2 ♘e6! **Black resigns**. If 2...fxe6, then 3 ♖xd7, so Black plays 2...♖xd1. Now comes the *zwischenzug*: 3 ♘xf8+ ♗xf8, and only then 4 ♖xd1.

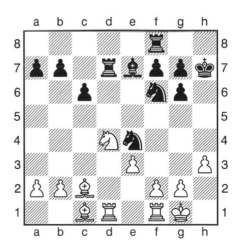

55

45 THE ♘g4 ZWISCHENZUG

Here is a fun pattern which begins with... a retreat! The white knight jumps backwards – unveiling an attack on the black queen. The true point is revealed next move, however – a *zwischenzug capture on f6*.

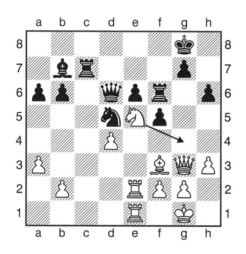

45a) White moves

Petkov-Kozhukharov
Bulgarian Ch, Pleven 2005

The unprotected black queen allows a surprising knight manoeuvre by White.

1 ♘g4! There is no time for Black to take the knight, due to the threat of 2 ♕xd6. But after 1...♕xg3 comes the *zwischenzug* **2 ♘xf6+**, winning an exchange: 2...♘xf6 3 fxg3.

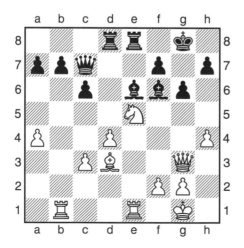

45b) White moves

Okhotnik-L.Bodrogi, Dunaujvaros 2005

Can you see the imaginative plan that wins at least a pawn in this position?

1 ♘g4! (if now 1...♕xg3, *two* zwischenzugs with check do the trick: 2 ♘xf6+ ♔g7 3 ♘xe8+!) **1...♕e7 2 ♖xb7!** (also 2 ♘xf6+ ♕xf6 3 ♖xb7) **2...♕xb7 3 ♘xf6+** and White wins.

THE ♘g6 ZWISCHENZUG

This theme has similarities with the previous
zwischenzug puzzle. But here the final target is
usually a *black rook or a black bishop* on the *e7-square*.

46a) White moves

Mainka-G.Reis, Nuremberg 2010

White's knight move works by *uncovering a threat of* ♕xd6, winning the black
queen.

1 ♘g6! Black is losing rook for knight.
On 1...♕xg3 comes the *zwischenzug* 2
♘xe7+, followed by 3 fxg3. And 1...♖d7
fails to 2 ♕xd6 ♖xd6 3 ♘e7+, forking
the other rook!

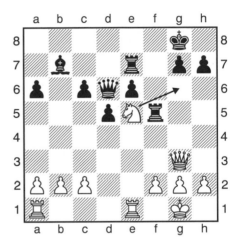

46b) Black moves

Delgado Ramirez-Cubas, Luque 2012

Now for an amazing mega-zwischen-
zug. How did Black stun his unsuspect-
ing opponent?

1...♘g3! White resigns. This beautiful
leap wins a piece due to a five-move sequence: 2 ♕xg6 ♖d1+! 3 ♔h2 ♘f1+ 4
♔g1 ♘xe3+ 5 ♔h2 ♘f1+ 6 ♔g1 fxg6.

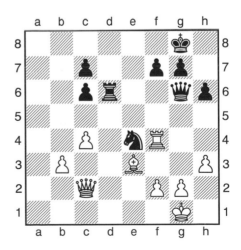

A MIGHTY MATE ON g8

This powerful checkmate pattern deserves more recognition.
It arises when the *white queen penetrates to the back rank*,
with *a knight in support on the e7-square*.

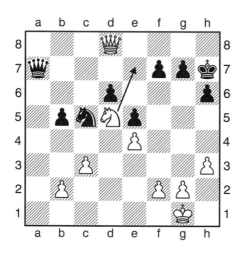

47a) White moves

Pikula-Kümin, Swiss League 2008

A simple knight move sets up the deadly mating-net.

1 ♘e7 Black resigns. The threat is 2 ♕g8 checkmate. If Black plays 1...h5, then 2 ♕g8+ ♔h6 gives White a choice of easy wins: 3 ♕h8+, 3 ♘f5+ or 3 ♕xf7.

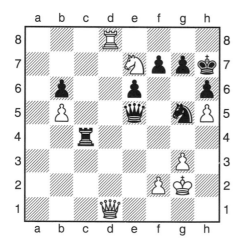

47b) White moves

Mashinskaya-Sirotkina
St Petersburg (women) 2000

White is a pawn down, and 1 ♕d3+ fails to 1...♕e4+. So how did she win?

1 ♖h8+! Black resigns. 1...♔xh8 is met by 2 ♕d8+ ♔h7 3 ♕g8 mate. White's rook sacrifice to win a tempo is routine procedure in this mating pattern.

Here the attacking queen and knight wreak havoc with the assistance of some *discovered checks*.

48a) Black moves

M.Mikadze-Abasov, Tbilisi 2007

Lots of checks – but how to mate? The trick is to relocate the knight to the e2-square.

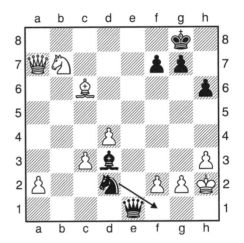

1...♘f1+ 2 ♔g1 ♘g3+! The knight is safe – the white king is in check from the black queen. **3 ♔h2 ♘e2 White resigns**. Mate can only be delayed: 4 h4 ♕g1+ 5 ♔h3 ♗f5+ 6 g4 ♗xg4 mate.

48b) White moves

M.Karthikeyan-G.Jaswant, Chennai 2011

Solid positions crumble in the face of discovered checks. How did White win?

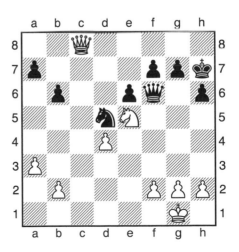

1 ♘d7 ♕f5 (remarkably, there is no safe square for the queen: 1...♕xd4 2 ♘f8+ ♔g8 3 ♘xe6+) **2 ♘f8+ ♔g8 3 ♘xe6+! Black resigns**. After 3...♔h7 the queen is lost to 4 ♘f8+ and 5 ♕xf5.

YOU *CAN* MATE WITH TWO KNIGHTS

There are several picturesque checkmates featuring two knights. These patterns do sometimes play a role in middlegame combinations, even if it is rare for the checkmates to occur on the board.

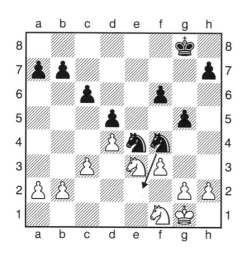

49a) Black moves

C.Schmitz-Tischendorf
Germany (teams) 2005/6

This shows one basic mating pattern. White has just played 1 f3, an unfortunate choice.

1...♘e2+ 2 ♔h1 ♘f2 checkmate.

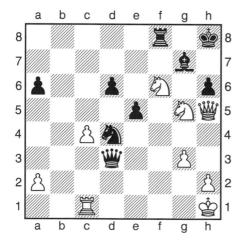

49b) White moves

B.Lengyel-Bokros, Balatonlelle 2005

Even if you see the idea, be careful! In one line Black has a surprising defence.

1 ♕e8! Black resigns. White threatens a beautiful checkmate by 2 ♘f7, which 1...♖xe8 doesn't prevent. The tempting 1 ♕f7? is a nice try, but Black can escape with 1...♕f3+! 2 ♘xf3 ♖xf7.

THE RAREST CHECKMATE

It is over 150 years since American Paul Morphy found this beautiful checkmate pattern with two knights. Since then it has occurred just a handful of times in serious competition.

50a) Black moves

Marache-Morphy
Blindfold simultaneous, New Orleans 1857

Black is doing well, but there is no hint of a unique two-knights mating pattern.

1...♘g3! White resigns. White's queen is attacked by the black queen, calling for the swap 2 ♕xg6. Instead of recapturing, a little piece of history is made: 2...♘de2 mate.

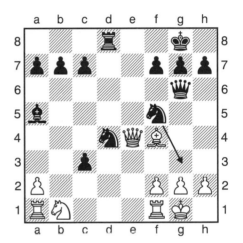

50b) Black moves

Bassler-Scheichel
European Junior Ch, Groningen 1971/2

Can you see a way to win the white queen using Morphy's idea?

1...♘xg3! White resigns. 2 ♘xf5 is met by 2...♘cxe2+!, when White can only get out of check by 3 ♕xe2, giving up his queen.

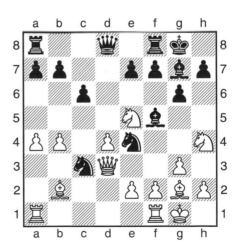

51 | BODEN & FRIENDS

The queenside checkmate pattern named after Samuel Boden
(1826-82) generates an endless supply of fresh victims.

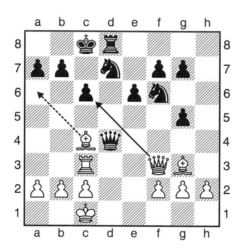

51a) White moves

Alavi-Wang Ting Hao
Asia Cup, Zaozhuang 2012

Unaware of the classic mating pattern,
Black has just captured a pawn on d4.

1 ♕xc6+! Black resigns. After 1...bxc6,
2 ♗a6 is a classic Boden's Mate.

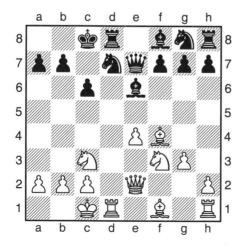

51b) White moves

Chalupnik-Solozhenkin, Gdynia 1989

How about this crazy version? Ask
yourself what move might give Black a
heart attack.

1 ♕a6! (threatening 2 ♕xc6+) **1...♕c5**
(1...bxa6 2 ♗xa6 is mate) **2 ♘a4 ♕e3+**
(or 2...♕f2 3 ♕xc6+) **3 ♗xe3 bxa6 4
♗xa6+** and White is winning.

ARABIAN KNIGHTS 52

This rook and knight checkmate pattern is known as the *Arabian Mate*. It is an important attacking theme, and arises in a wide range of settings.

52a) White moves

Karpov-Stojanović, Valjevo 2007

Anatoly Karpov, former World Champion, is not going to miss this two-mover.

1 ♕xh6+! gxh6 2 ♖g8 checkmate.

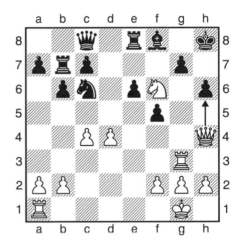

52b) Black moves

Kariakin-Vallejo Pons, Cuernavaca 2006

A simple endgame – yet Black can win by force. How?

1...♖g5 White resigns. The Arabian mate (2...♖g1) must be prevented. But after 2 ♖g2 ♖xg2 3 ♔xg2 ♘e1+ Black carries out a *knight fork* of the white king and bishop.

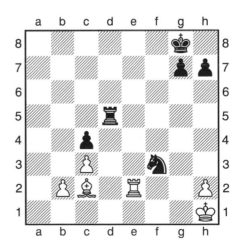

53 REMEMBER THE ROOK-LIFT

A serious attack on the enemy king often benefits from a *rook-lift*.
This is where your rook moves forwards – with the aim of
then transferring sideways, to a more aggressive location.

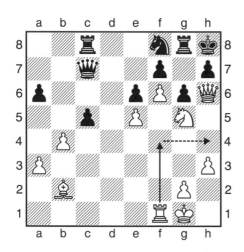

53a) White moves

Radjabov-V.Alcazar
World Under-12 Ch, Oropesa del Mar 1998

The black defence is just about holding
– until a *rook-lift* takes place.

1 ♖f4 Black resigns. The white rook is
headed sideways for the h-file, and
Black is helpless; e.g., 1...♕d7 2 ♖h4
and mate looms with 3 ♕xh7+ ♘xh7 4
♖xh7.

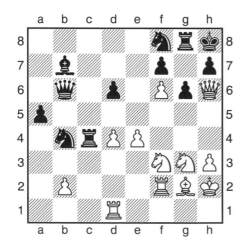

53b) White moves

Davies-Hendriks, London 2009

White has conducted a textbook attack.
How does he now finish Black off?

1 ♘g5 ♕c7 (to stop 2 ♘xf7 mate) **2
♖f4** (the rook-lift) **2...♖c2 3 ♖g1** (can-
celling out tricks with 3...♖xg2+ and
4...♕c2+) **Black resigns**. Next move
White has 4 ♖h4, or even 4 ♘xh7.

ROOK-LIFT WITH ♖f5

This is a super-aggressive rook-lift where White advances his rook to f5 – *even though that square is defended*. This manoeuvre can break down even a quite solid defensive structure.

54a) White moves

Perpinya-Bernabe Duran, Murcia 1997

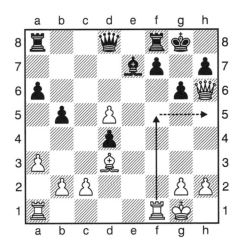

White wants to relocate his f1-rook to the h-file. But how, as 1 ♖f3 ♗g5 favours Black?

1 ♖f5! A great way to bring the rook into the attack. 1...gxf5 gets mated: 2 ♗xf5 ♖e8 3 ♕xh7+ ♔f8 4 ♕h8. **1...♗f6 2 ♖h5! ♖e8 3 ♖f1 Black resigns**. White's attack is too strong.

54b) Black moves

Karlsson-J.Gonzalez Garcia, Sitges 2010

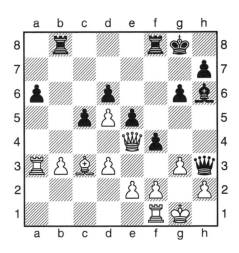

Both sides have well-placed pieces, yet Black can win by force. How?

1...f3! (threatening 2...♕g2 mate) **2 exf3 ♖f4! 3 gxf4** (if 3 ♕e2 ♖h4 4 gxh4 ♗f4, it is mate in two) **3...♗xf4** and the only way to struggle on was with **4 ♕xf4**, giving up the queen.

SMOTHERED & SEMI-SMOTHERED MATE

The patterns below don't occur often, but they are still useful to know. Also, they are two of the prettiest checkmates – provided you are on the right side of them.

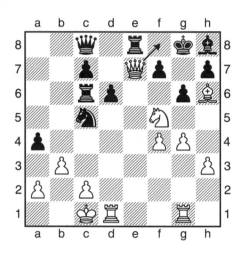

55a) White moves

Maderna-Co.Bauer, La Plata 1927

This version could be easily missed. Note how the black bishop takes away an escape-square from the black king.

1 ♕f8+! Black resigns. White's queen is attractively sacrificed on an empty square. After 1...♖xf8, 2 ♘e7 is checkmate.

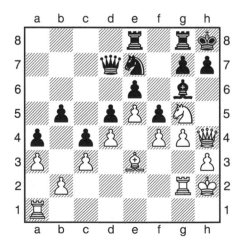

55b) White moves

Carvajal-C.A.Hernandez, Santa Rosa 2011

This smothered mate pattern should be more obvious. Can you spot the two-move win?

1 ♕xh7+! ♗xh7 2 ♘f7 checkmate.

A CLASSIC
SEMI-SMOTHERED MATE

This semi-smothered mate – where White ignores an attack on the queen – has been around for over a century. World Champion Wilhelm Steinitz won a game with the idea in New York 1894.

56a) White moves

Zufić-Janković
Croatian Team Ch, Šibenik 2007

Black's last move, ...♕d8-f8, was intended to eject the white queen from its attacking position.

1 ♘g5! This response is very strong. The threat is 2 ♕xh7 mate, and if Black takes the queen, we see an elegant conclusion: 1...♕xh6 2 ♘xf7 mate.

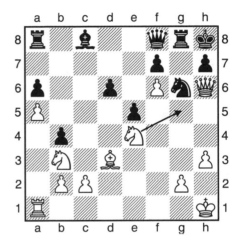

56b) White moves

Berczes-S.Widmer, Biel 2005

What deadly three-move finish has Black overlooked?

1 ♘h3 (White's knight sets off for g5) **1...♕h5 2 ♘g5! Black resigns**. There is no defence to the threatened 3 ♘xf7 checkmate.

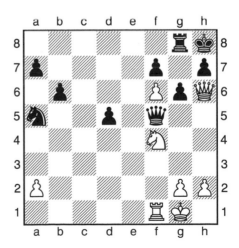

57 A QUEEN SACRIFICE ON h7

The puzzles below feature a notable mating pattern with a queen sacrifice. A key ingredient is the *white pawn on f5*, which stops the black king escaping to the g6-square.

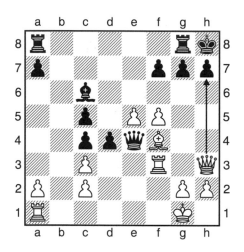

57a) White moves

R.Tauber-M.Grimm, Germany (teams) 2003/4

The black king on h8 is hemmed in. So White opens the h-file with a queen sacrifice.

1 ♛xh7+! Black resigns. After the forced 1...♚xh7, a waiting white rook delivers checkmate with 2 ♖h3. Black's king has no escape – the g6-square is covered by the white pawn on f5.

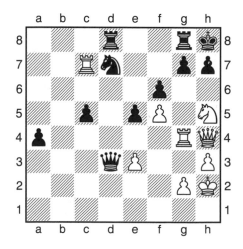

57b) White moves

Wang Hao-Roktim, Asian Ch, Hyderabad 2005

A brilliant move decides the game. Can you find it?

1 ♘f4! A lovely concept, made possible by the queen-sacrifice variation 1...exf4 2 ♛xh7+ ♚xh7 3 ♖h4 checkmate. Black tried **1...♛xf5**, but lost his queen to **2 ♘g6+ ♛xg6 3 ♖xg6**.

OFF TO THE BEACH

Gain some extra sunbathing time with this bishop & knight checkmate pattern, right in the opening...

58a) Black moves

Jiruse-Kr.Georgiev, Sunny Beach 2011

A quick finish from the tournament held in Bulgaria's biggest Black Sea holiday resort.

1...♛xd5! 2 cxd5 ♘f3+ 3 ♔f1 ♝h3 checkmate.

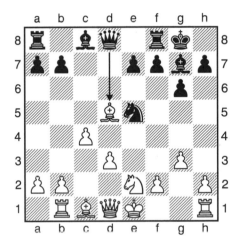

58b) Black moves

Peev-Haïk, Bucharest 1979

A startling move wins Black a pawn or two. Any guesses?

1...♛f3! 2 ♝b1 (the attacked bishop retreats, since 2 gxf3 ♘xf3+ 3 ♔f1 ♝h3 is mate) **2...♛xg2 3 ♔d2 ♛xf2** Having started a pawn down in the diagram position, Black is now one ahead.

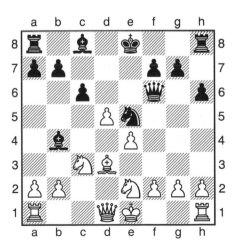

ATTACKING THE UNCASTLED KING

If an opponent is slow in getting castled, there are techniques to make life uncomfortable for a king in the centre. Typical focal points for attention are the *e6-, f7- and g6-squares*.

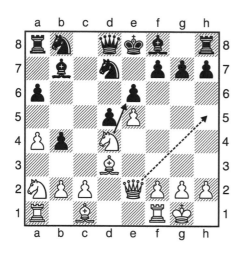

59a) White moves

Opening Trap, Sicilian Kan variation

A knight sacrifice opens the h5-e8 diagonal for White's follow-up queen check.

1 ♘xe6! fxe6 2 ♕h5+ ♔e7 After 2...g6 3 ♗xg6+ hxg6 4 ♕xg6+ ♔e7 5 ♗g5+ White wins outright. **3 ♗g5+ ♘f6 4 exf6+ gxf6 5 ♗xf6+! ♔xf6 6 ♕h4+** and the black queen is lost to a *skewer*.

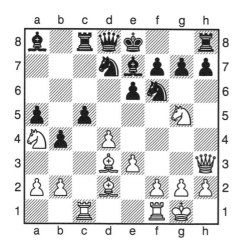

59b) White moves

Fressinet-N.Brunner, French League 2011

What shock move causes the black position to disintegrate?

1 ♗g6! (as on 1...fxg6 or 1...♖f8, the black queen is lost to 2 ♘xe6) **1...0-0** (or 1...hxg6 2 ♕xh8+) **2 ♗xh7+ ♔h8 3 dxc5** White is a pawn up, with multiple attacking threats.

A ♖xe6 SACRIFICE

Here is a novel pattern that arises in some specific opening systems.
First *a rook sacrifice* exposes the black king. Then the
white queen and knight cooperate in a decisive assault.

60a) White moves

Opening Trap, Caro-Kann Defence

Black has just swapped bishops on g2,
expecting a routine recapture with 1
♔xg2.

1 ♖xe6+! fxe6 2 ♕h5+ ♔e7 Or 2...♔d8
3 ♘xe6+, forking the black king and
queen. **3 ♕f7+** White wins after 3...♔d8
4 ♘xe6+.

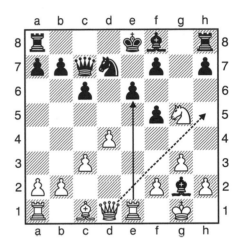

60b) White moves

Bojkov-G.Festas
Greek Team Ch, Kallithea 2008

This game started as a Scandinavian Defence (1 e4 d5). What strong continuation does White have here?

1 ♘g5 (threatening 2 f3, as well as 2
♘xe4, winning a pawn) **1...♗xg2 2
♖xe6+! ♔f8 3 ♕h5 Black resigns.**

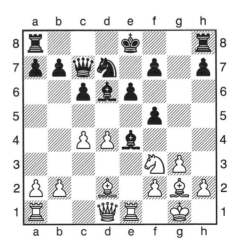

71

A RARE & DEEP DISCOVERY

In this sophisticated pattern, a white knight is sacrificed to *decoy the black king to f7*. This is so a pawn capture (dxe6) is *check* – and this in turn unveils a discovered attack down the long diagonal. Simple!

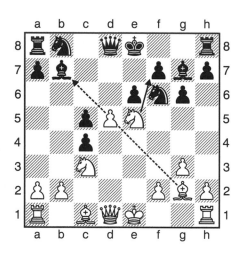

61a) White moves

Kustar-Izoria, Berkeley 2008

White uses the theme to catch out a grandmaster opponent rated 250 points higher.

1 ♘xf7! The point is that 1...♔xf7 2 dxe6+ is *check*, and so 3 ♗xb7 next move will win White material. The game went **1...♕e7 2 ♘xh8 exd5+ 3 ♕e2** with a white advantage.

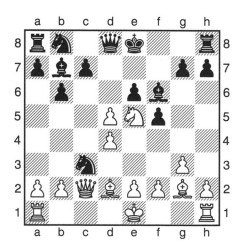

61b) White moves

Aronian-Navara, Turin Olympiad 2006

White tries an amazing concept – can you see the idea?

1 ♘f7! ♕d7? (if 1...♔xf7?, then 2 dxe6+ followed by 3 ♗xb7, but the best defence is 1...♕c8! 2 ♘xh8 ♘xd5) **2 ♗xc3! ♗xd5** (any capture on f7 still loses to 3 dxe6) **3 ♗xd5 ♕xd5 4 e4! fxe4 5 ♘xh8** with a winning position.

PRISING OPEN THE a-FILE

This smart bishop move wins either an exchange (rook for bishop) – or the defender must relinquish his queen. By *forcing open the a-file*, White creates *a discovered attack on the black rook on a8*.

62a) White moves

Pilecki-Czyrson, Gdansk Ch 2003

White pins the black queen against the black king. So Black is forced to capture the bishop.

1 ♗b5! axb5 2 axb5 The black queen is still under attack – and now so also is the black rook on a8. White has the advantage, due the double threat of 3 bxc6 and 3 ♖xa8+.

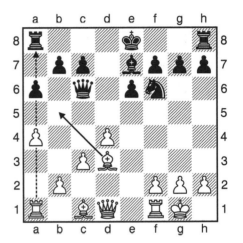

62b) White moves

M.Khassanov-J.Berry
Canadian Ch, Brantford 1999

Black, an experienced campaigner, had overlooked something. What was it?

1 ♗b6! axb6 2 axb6 ♕xb6 (having a rook on d8 proves unfortunate for Black: 2...♖xa1 3 bxc7 ♖xc1 4 cxd8♕+) **3 ♖xa8** White is rook for bishop ahead.

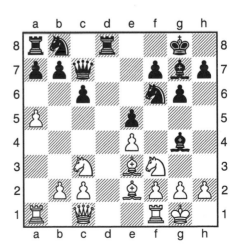

DISCOVERED ATTACK ON THE c-FILE

In a *discovered attack*, a piece moves to uncover
an attack from another piece. This version can win
you anything – from a pawn to a queen.

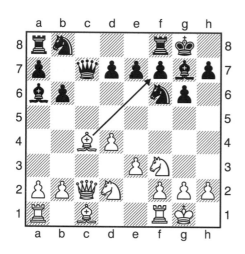

63a) White moves

Montoliu Costa-Benavent Espi
Cullera 2009

From an amateur game. Black falls for a
discovered attack – and loses his queen.

1 ♗xf7+! Black resigns. White sacrificed the bishop *with check* to clear a
path to the black queen. Black must deal
with the check, e.g. 1...♖xf7, where-
upon 2 ♕xc7 wins.

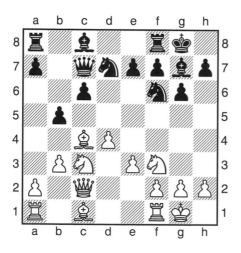

63b) White moves

Korchnoi-Kakageldiev
Dresden Olympiad 2008

How did 'Viktor the Terrible' win a
pawn in this position?

1 ♘xb5! ♕b8 (if the knight is captured,
a discovered attack will cost Black his
queen: 1...cxb5? 2 ♗xf7+!) **2 ♘c3** and
White was simply a pawn ahead.

DISCOVERED ATTACK WITH ♖g4+

Would you like to win a queen (worth nine pawns) for a rook (worth five pawns)? Stay alert for this occasional *discovered attack* theme.

64a) White moves

Batyte-S.Misović
European Women's Teams, Khersonissos 2007

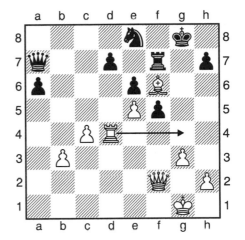

The black king position is just slightly exposed – but one check is all it takes.

1 ♖g4+! It transpires the black queen is unfortunately placed. **1...fxg4 2 ♕xa7 Black resigns**. White has given up a rook, but won a more valuable queen in return.

64b) White moves

Naumkin-Scipioni, Porto San Giorgio 2008

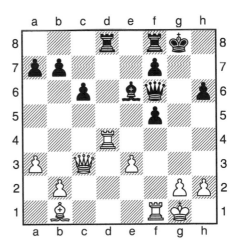

How did White, a Russian grandmaster, end the game immediately?

1 ♖g4+! Black resigns. The black queen on f6 is lost. If 1...fxg4, White even has a choice of ways to capture, 2 ♕xf6 or 2 ♖xf6.

AMAZING DISCOVERIES

A *discovered attack* is often combined with other motifs,
like *breaking a pin*. For an especially pretty finish,
let's throw in a checkmating pattern too.

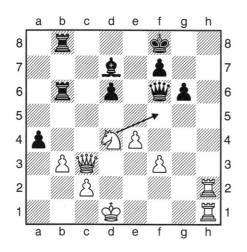

65a) White moves

Cederstam-B.Arjun, Stockholm 2011/12

White's unexpected knight leap snares
the black king in a mating formation.

1 ♘f5! Black resigns. A *discovered attack* on the black queen means White
threatens 2 ♕xf6. But if 1...♕xc3 it is
mate in two moves: 2 ♖h8+ ♕xh8 3
♖xh8.

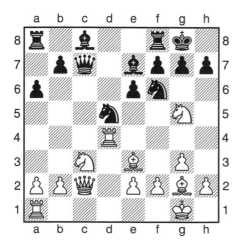

65b) White moves

Ni Hua-Adly, Shenzhen 2011

This beautiful combination caught out
a grandmaster. Can you find the win?

1 ♘xd5! Black resigns. Too late, Black
sees the idea: 1...♕xc2 (if 1...♘xd5, 2
♕xh7 mate) 2 ♘xe7+ ♔h8 3 ♘xf7+
♖xf7 4 ♖d8+ with a back-rank mate in
two more moves.

CARNAGE ON THE CHESSBOARD

Every year hundreds – if not thousands – of players needlessly fall for these routine ♘d5 discovered attack traps. Please be careful out there.

66a) White moves

H.Kunkel-Dettweiler
Germany (teams) 2010/11

White's knight move uncovers a *discovered attack against the black queen*.

1 ♘d5! Black resigns. 1...♛xd2 (or else the black queen is lost; e.g., 1...cxd5 2 ♛xa5) 2 ♘xe7 checkmate.

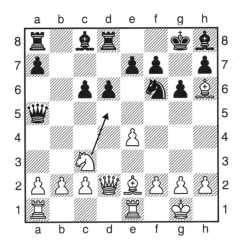

66b) White moves

Barrionuevo-L.Mavrich, Villa Martelli 2007

Analyse three moves ahead and show how White wins a piece for nothing.

1 ♘d5! ♛xd2 2 ♘xe7+ (the *zwischenzug* that catches out so many players: before recapturing the queen, White takes a piece *with check*) **2...♚h8 3 ♘xd2 Black resigns**.

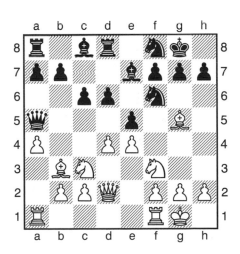

A NEAT WAY TO WIN A ROOK

This cunning theme uses an imaginative queen swap... to win a rook! It incorporates the motif of *discovered attack*.

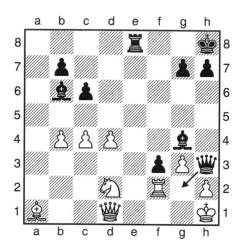

67a) Black moves

Schallopp-Blackburne, London 1885

'The Black Death' lives up to his nickname with a temporary queen sacrifice.

1...♛g2+! White resigns. On 2 ♖xg2 the recapture 2...fxg2+ gives *check* – and is also a *discovered attack on the white queen*. Black goes a rook ahead after 3 ♔xg2 ♗xd1.

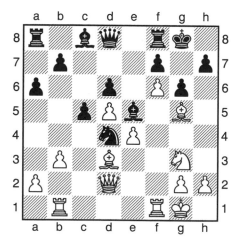

67b) White moves

Barnaure-Nanu, Bucharest 2007

With a creative idea, White won this position in just three moves. Can you see how?

1 ♗h4! ♔h8 2 ♕h6 ♖g8 3 ♕g7+ Black resigns.

A SUSCEPTIBLE STRUCTURE

The two positions below both feature a black kingside formation with *pawns on f7, g7 and g6*. While not a terrible structure, it is vulnerable to rook & knight back-rank combinations.

68a) White moves

Grachev-Inarkiev, Moscow 2011

White's rook and knight launch a mating attack – courtesy of a queen sacrifice.

1 ♖xd6! ♕xc2 2 ♖d8+ ♔h7 3 ♘g5+ Black resigns. After 3...♔h6 4 ♘xf7+ ♔h7 (4...♔h5 5 ♖h8+), 5 ♖h8 is checkmate.

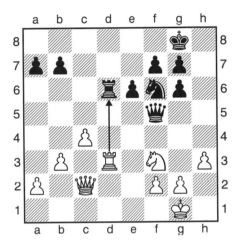

68b) White moves

Turutin-Gorbatov, Zvenigorod 2008

Can there really be a win for White here? You'll need to work hard to solve this one.

1 ♕c8+! ♖xc8 2 ♖xc8+ ♔h7 3 ♗e3! **♕xe3** (3...♘xe3 4 ♘g5+ sets up a mating-net: 4...♔h6 5 ♘xf7+ and 6 ♖h8 mate) **4 fxe3** and White won the ending.

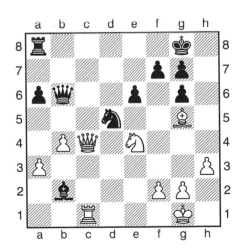

SNOOZE & LOSE

Any momentary lapse of attention can be fatal with back-rank combinations, as they occur very suddenly.
Here are two different patterns to watch out for.

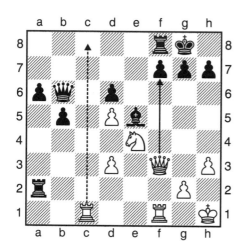

69a) White moves

R.Mitrović-Ravić, Belgrade 2012

White's checkmate finish (against a much stronger opponent) is a well-known theme.

1 ♕xf7+! Black resigns. After 1...♖xf7 White delivers checkmate with 2 ♖c8+; e.g., 2...♖f8 3 ♖(either)xf8.

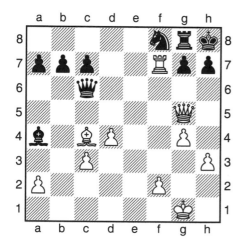

69b) White moves

V.Denisov-Kurdakov, Moscow 2012

One of several patterns with a king in the corner. White checkmates in three moves.

1 ♕xg7+! Black resigns. The forced finish is 1...♖xg7 2 ♖xf8+ ♖g8 3 ♖xg8 checkmate.

In this back-rank ruse, an attacking queen, rook and bishop cooperate in a fast and forcing checkmate. The sequence is four moves long, and not always obvious. Stay alert!

70a) White moves

Fitzsimons-R.Griffiths, Dun Laoghaire 2010

Black is ahead on material, but has over-looked a standard checkmate theme.

1 ♕xf7+! ♖xf7 2 ♖d8+ ♖f8 3 ♗d5+ ♔h8 4 ♖xf8 mate.

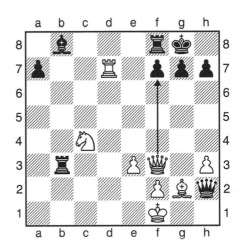

70b) Black moves

Moiseenko-Yusupov
European Rapidplay Ch, Warsaw 2010

Grandmaster Yusupov knew the mating pattern – do you?

1...♕xf2+! 2 ♖xf2 ♖b1+ White resigns. Since 3 ♖f1 ♗e3+ 4 ♔h1 ♖xf1+ 5 ♘g1 ♖xg1 is mate.

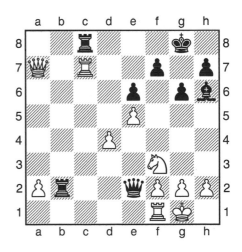

71 BACK-RANK BRILLIANCE

This checkmate pattern involves a queen and two rooks. With the black king in the corner, the white queen is sacrificed on g7. The purpose is to *deflect a defending black rook off the back rank*.

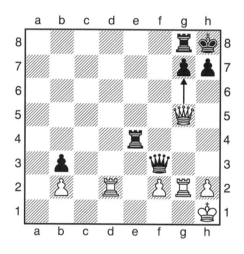

71a) White moves

K.Berg-Kaiszauri, Copenhagen 1982

Black assumed he was winning here, having completely overlooked White's threat.

1 ♕xg7+! Black resigns. If 1...♖xg7, capturing the queen, White can deliver checkmate in at most four moves: 2 ♖d8+ ♖e8 3 ♖xe8+ ♕f8 4 ♖xf8+ ♖g8 5 ♖(either)xg8 mate.

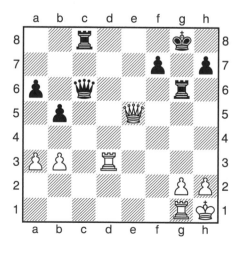

71b) Black moves

I.Martinez-O.Jakobsen
Thessaloniki Olympiad 1984

In positional terms, White is well centralized. Tactically he has a problem. Can you see it?

1...♕xg2+! White resigns. After 2 ♖xg2, 2...♖c1+ forces checkmate in three moves.

A PAWN-ON-THE-SEVENTH TRICK 72

A pawn on the seventh rank – one square from promotion – makes back-rank combinations more likely. Our theme here can easily deceive, as the killer bank-rank blow comes from a surprise direction.

72a) White moves

Playa-Masserey
World Junior Ch, Buenos Aires 1992

Controlling the only open file doesn't save Black from this non-standard mate.

1 f7+! ♔h8 (if 1...♖xf7, 2 ♕a8+) **2 ♕a8! Black resigns**. Unexpectedly, the white queen arrives on the back rank via the diagonal. On 2...♖xa8, 3 f8♕+ will mate or if 2...♕xf7, 3 ♕xf8+.

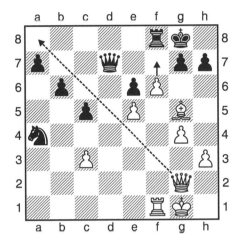

72b) White moves

Gurgenidze-Spassky
USSR Team Ch, Moscow 1959

White played 1 fxg7 and only drew. What win did he famously miss in the diagram position?

1 f7+! ♔h8 (or 1...♖axf7 2 ♖xf7 ♖xf7 3 ♕d8+) **2 ♕d8!** would have led to forced mate.

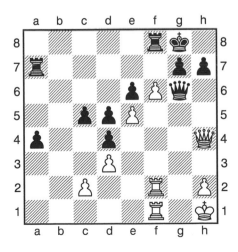

83

73 | ROOK & QUEEN DOUBLE-ACT

This checkmate pattern normally forces mate in three moves. White needs *a pawn on the f6-square* and *a rook on the opponent's back rank*. The final ingredient – *a queen pointed at the h6-square*.

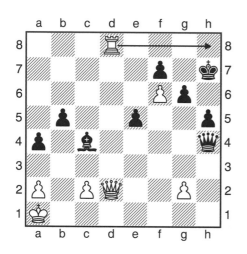

73a) White moves

Aravindh-J.Herman
World Junior Ch, Chennai 2011

A rook sacrifice gives the white queen access to the h6-square.

1 ♖h8+! Black resigns. After 1...♔xh8, 2 ♕h6+ ♔g8 3 ♕g7 is checkmate.

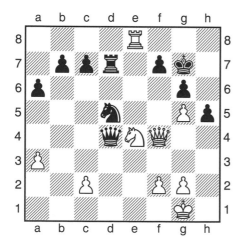

73b) White moves

B.Mendoza-Perena, Tagaytay City 2010

Here White established the mating pattern with a tactical flourish. How?

1 ♘f6! (bravo! White's queen is twice attacked, but a ♖g8 Arabian mate is threatened) **1...♘xf6 2 gxf6+ ♔h7** (2...♕xf6 3 ♖g8+ costs Black a queen) **3 ♖h8+! Black resigns**.

84

THE TRIPLE-ACT

This disguised (and equally deadly) version of the
previous mate pattern is often overlooked. A long-range bishop
provides support for the attacking rook & queen.

74a) Black moves

J.Mädler-Uhlmann
East German Ch, Aschersleben 1963

A pioneering combination from Black,
an 11-times East German Champion.

1...♖h1+! White resigns. After 2 ♘xh1,
2...♕xg2 is mate, or if 2 ♔xh1, then
2...♕h3+! (the g2-pawn is pinned by
the black bishop) 3 ♔g1 ♕xg2 mate.

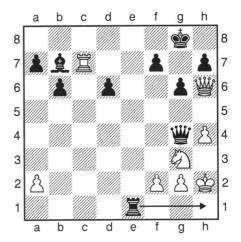

74b) Black moves

Zhao Xue-Cmilyte
Russian Women's Team Ch, Dagomys 2010

How did the game end? There are *two*
defences Black needs to break down.

1...♖h1+! 2 ♔g3 (2 ♔xh1 ♕xh3+ 3
♔g1 ♕xg2 mate is clear enough)
2...♗xg2! White resigns. If 3 ♔xg2,
3...♕xh3 is checkmate.

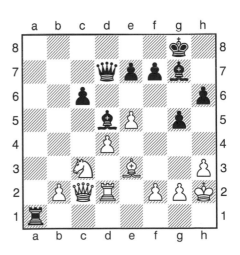

75 THE CLASSIC ROOK DEFLECTION

A chance appears to swap some heavy pieces. An
endgame is coming, the defender relaxes.
Big mistake – this rook deflection will cost serious material.

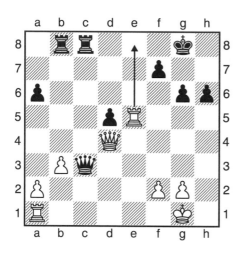

75a) White moves

V.Sanal-C.Burcu
Turkish Team Ch, Konya 2011

Black has just captured a pawn on c3, expecting a queen swap and a draw.

1 ♖e8+! Black resigns. A deflecting sacrifice wins on the spot. If 1...♖xe8 2 ♕xc3 the black queen is lost. If 1...♔h7 the simplest is 2 ♕xc3 ♖xc3 3 ♖xb8, winning a rook.

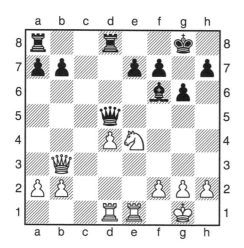

75b) White moves

Shytaj-F.Levin, Bratto 2008

This version trapped a grandmaster. How did White win?

1 ♘xf6+ exf6 2 ♖e8+! Black resigns. A queen is lost in the line 2...♖xe8 3 ♕xd5, or a rook is lost after 2...♔g7 3 ♕xd5 ♖xd5 4 ♖xa8.

A *deflection* causes a defending piece to be overloaded.
In the two puzzles below, a defender's rook is overloaded –
distracted from the vital task of protecting his queen.

76a) Black moves

Bj.Thorfinnsson-Nayer
European Clubs Cup, Fügen 2006

A Russian grandmaster shows his class.

1...♖e1+! White resigns. Very pretty.
The white queen is lost after 2 ♖xe1
♕xd3, as the bishop on f2 is pinned and
cannot assist.

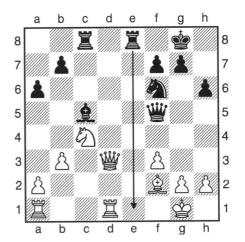

76b) White moves

Radulsky-Argiroudis, Blagoevgrad 2010

White deliberately gave up his c4-pawn
to reach this position. Why?

1 ♖d8+! Black resigns. If 1...♖xd8,
then 2 ♕xc4, while 1...♗xd8 allows 2
♕e8 checkmate.

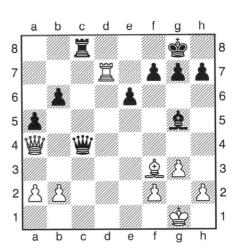

77 IN THE FOOTSTEPS OF ALEKHINE

Former World Champion Alexander Alekhine had a wonderful eye for a combination. In 1925, he showed how a particular pawn-formation could be vulnerable to an attack with queen and rooks.

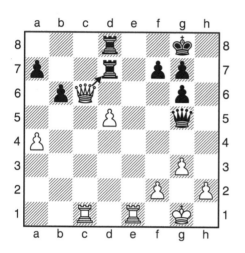

77a) White moves

Alekhine-Colle, Paris 1925

Although h7 is an escape-square for the black king, a back-rank combination is still possible.

1 ♕xd7! ♖xd7 2 ♖e8+ ♔h7 3 ♖cc8 ♖d8 4 ♖exd8 Black resigns. The threat of 5 ♖h8 checkmate is decisive.

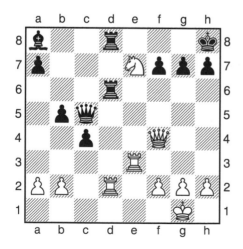

77b) White moves

Mamedyarov-Timofeev, Moscow 2004

First find a remarkable sacrifice...

1 ♘g6+! hxg6 (1...fxg6 is met by 2 ♕xd6!; e.g., 2...♖xd6 3 ♖e8 mate) **2 ♕h4+ ♕h5** (2...♔g8 3 ♕xd8+! ♖xd8 4 ♖xd8+ ♔h7 5 ♖h3+) **3 ♕xd8+! ♖xd8 4 ♖xd8+ ♔h7 5 ♖ee8 Black resigns**.

LEARNING FROM HISTORY

78

The full version of this theme is long-known (for example from the game Frydman-Vidmar, Ujpest 1934). If you haven't seen the combination before, prepare to be amazed.

78a) White moves

Napoli-G.Altea, Laconi 2007

First, a simple version. The black knight has one too many defensive tasks...

1 ♗xh7+! Black resigns. Black's queen is lost after either 1...♘xh7 2 ♕xd7 or 1...♔h8 2 ♗f5+ (giving a *discovered check* from the white queen) 2...♔g8 3 ♗xd7.

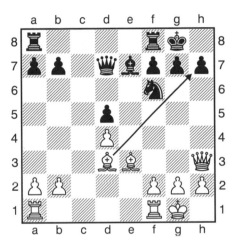

78b) White moves

Fe.Fernandez-Carlo Miranda
Pan American Junior Ch, Cali 2010

The Full Monty. Can you spot White's extraordinary first move?

1 ♘xd5! (striking; yes, 1...♘xd5? 2 ♕xh7 is mate – but isn't d5 defended by a black pawn?) **1...exd5 2 ♘xd7** Black cannot recapture: 2...♕xd7 3 ♗xh7+!.

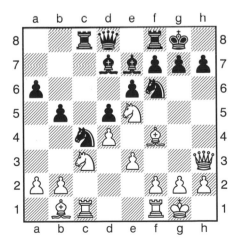

89

PAWN-GRAB ON THE h7-SQUARE

Normally the chess expression 'pawn-grab' implies taking some risk to win material. Not here! White captures the h7-pawn totally for free, despite it being apparently defended.

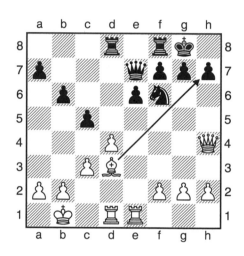

79a) White moves

Thorgeirsson-E.Thorsteinsson
Reykjavik 2010

The h7-pawn is protected by the black knight. Normally fine – but here the knight is *pinned*.

1 ♗xh7+! This wins a pawn, as 1...♘xh7 allows 2 ♕xe7, capturing the black queen. After **1...♔h8 2 ♗c2+ ♔g8 3 ♖e3** White won quickly.

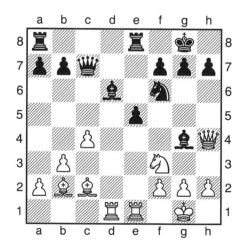

79b) White moves

Abramović-S.Elez, Banja Luka 2004

How can White win a pawn for nothing in this position?

1 ♗xh7+! (this time the target is the black bishop on g4) **1...♘xh7 2 ♕xg4.**

90

MORE FREE PAWNS

The same basic theme as the puzzles on the opposite page –
but here the pawn-win is more deeply concealed.

80a) Black moves

Gelabert-B.Vega Gutierrez
Spanish Ch, Palma de Mallorca 2009

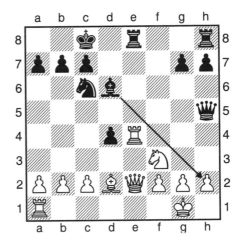

Here a pawn-grab works even though the white queen is guarded by a rook.

1...♗xh2+! As on 2 ♘xh2 ♕xe2 Black wins using a rare X-ray motif: 3 ♖xe2 ♖xe2. In the game White struggled on with **2 ♔f1**, a pawn down.

80b) White moves

Savon-Lunev, Oriol 1997

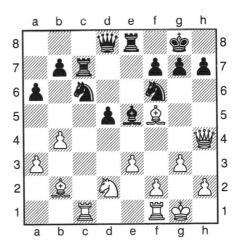

There is a neat pawn-win hidden here, but you'll need to defeat two defences...

1 ♗xe5 ♘xe5 (1...♖xe5 fails to the twin line 2 ♗xh7+! ♘xh7 3 ♕xd8+ ♘xd8 4 ♖xc7) **2 ♗xh7+!** ♔f8 (White's idea is 2...♘xh7 3 ♕xd8 ♖xd8 4 ♖xc7) **3 ♗f5** and White is a pawn ahead.

THE UBIQUITOUS GREEK GIFT

You probably know the *Greek Gift* sacrifice. A white bishop is given up in return for a concerted attack using queen & knight.
Many versions win, a few versions lose, and some are unclear!

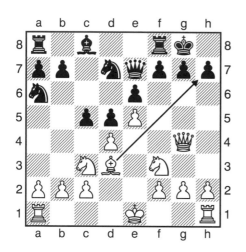

81a) White moves

Bakoyannis-P.Doulidis
Greek Team Ch, Eretria 2011

Even the locals can fall for the most basic of gifts. This version wins for sure.

1 ♗xh7+! ♔xh7 2 ♕h5+ Black resigns. After 2...♔g8, 3 ♘g5 is crushing, due to the checkmate threat of 4 ♕h7. For example, 3...♖e8 4 ♕h7+ ♔f8 5 ♕h8 mate.

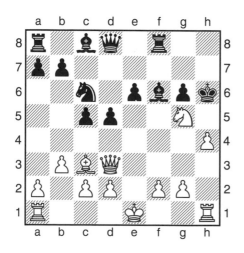

81b) White moves

Rendle-F.Guido, Bratto 2005

Three moves into a bold Greek Gift sacrifice, find the one move that keeps the attack alive.

1 h5! ♘e7 (the threat was 2 ♕xg6 mate; 1...gxh5 2 ♕h7+ ♔xg5 3 ♕xh5+ leads to a quick mate) **2 ♘f7+ ♖xf7 3 hxg6+ Black resigns**. 3...♔g7 4 ♖h7+ decides.

THE CUNNING ♘xd7 TRAP

This ploy exploits a potential *skewer* of the black queen and rook. White makes a knight swap on the d7-square – and it transpires that Black has no good recapture. White wins at least a pawn.

82a) White moves

Nayer-Milman, New York (rapidplay) 2002

Since this game, several players have fallen for this exact opening trap.

1 ♘xd7 Now Black sees the problem: if 1...♕xd7, 2 ♗f5 skewers his queen and rook. So he captures with the knight. **1...♘xd7 2 ♗xh7+** White has won a pawn for nothing.

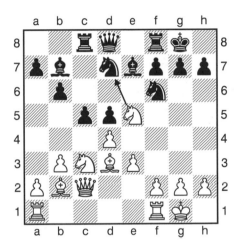

82b) White moves

Kantsler-A.Krasevec, Ljubljana 1992

Black looks super-solid. Yet play your moves in the right order, and you will be rewarded...

1 ♗xf6 ♗xf6 2 ♘xd7 ♕xd7 3 ♗f5! **♘e6 4 ♗xh7+** The h7-pawn falls. Remarkable, given it was defended three times in the diagram position!

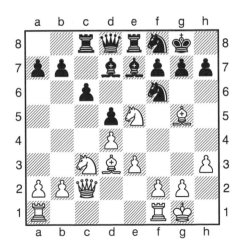

KEEP CONTROL
WITH ♕h6

Could you resist capturing a free h7-pawn with check?
This manoeuvre requires self-control –
but will stop the enemy king escaping.

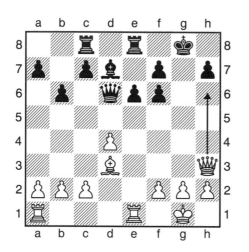

83a) White moves

Tarrasch-Mieses
Match game 3, Berlin 1916

If 1 ♕xh7+ ♔f8, the black king runs for shelter to the e7-square.

1 ♕h6! Very elegant – now the king is hemmed in. 1...f5 To stop 2 ♗xh7+. 2 ♖e3 ♕xd4 3 c3 Black resigns. As 4 ♖g3+ is coming next move.

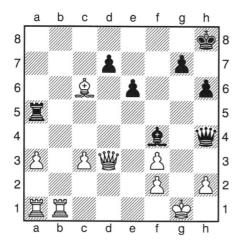

83b) Black moves

Kazantsev-Kersten, Budapest 1995

After 1...♖g5+ (or 1...♕xh2+) 2 ♔f1 the white king escapes. What to do?

1...♕h3! (suddenly White is defenceless) 2 ♖b5 ♗xh2+ 3 ♔h1 ♗g3+ White resigns. A typical mate will follow: 4 ♔g1 ♕h2+ 5 ♔f1 ♕xf2 mate.

94

HORT'S NIFTY SIDESTEP 84

So you have managed to expose the enemy king – but how to finish him off? This finesse might come in useful...

84a) White moves

Baumhus-Konikowski
German League 1987/8

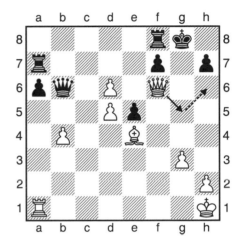

The immediate 1 ♕h6 gives Black time to defend with 1...f6. So time for a sidestep.

1 ♕g5+! ♔h8 2 ♕h6 Black resigns. Due to White's neat manoeuvre, there are now *two* mate threats. Black cannot cope with both 3 ♕xh7 *and* 3 ♕xf8.

84b) White moves

Hort-Portisch, Madrid 1973

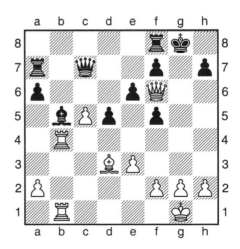

How did Grandmaster Hort win by force in just three moves?

1 ♖g4+! fxg4 (the rook sacrifice has opened the b1-h7 diagonal; now for the sidestep) **2 ♕g5+! ♔h8 3 ♕h6 Black resigns.** There is no time for 3...♗xd3 due to 4 ♕xf8 mate.

SIMPLE PERPETUAL
WITH A QUEEN

A *perpetual check* is a draw, because otherwise one side could keep checking forever. The draw can be claimed as a three-fold repetition of position, but in practice the players see it coming, and agree a draw.

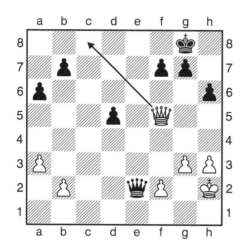

85a) White moves

Dizdarević-Atalik, Zenica 2006

White is a pawn down, but can force a draw with a routine perpetual check.

1 ♕c8+ ♔h7 2 ♕f5+ ♔g8 Draw agreed. The white queen just keeps checking. Black must acquiesce, as 2...g6 allows 3 ♕xf7+.

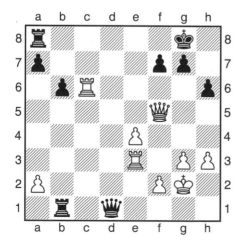

85b) White moves

Frade-Marques – Flouzat
French League 2002/3

The white king is in grave danger. How would you escape with a draw?

1 ♖c8+ ♖xc8 2 ♕xc8+ ♔h7 3 ♕f5+ ♔g8 4 ♕c8+ ♔h7 Draw agreed.

THE STANDARD QUEEN PERPETUAL

This is perhaps the most common perpetual-check draw of all.
The white queen alternates *between the h5-square
and the e8-square, repeatedly checking the black king.*

86a) White moves

Zhou Jianchao-Ye Rongguang
Wuxi (teams) 2005

Worried by his opponent's far-advanced c-pawn, White forces a draw by perpetual check.

1 ♕e8+ ♔h7 2 ♕h5+ ♔g8 Draw agreed. The queen checks will be repeated indefinitely.

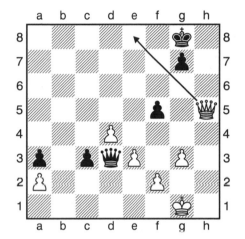

86b) White moves

J.Vojinović-B.Hund
European Women's Teams, Khersonissos 2007

Black threatens 1...♕xg2 mate. How did White cleverly save the draw?

1 ♘g5+! hxg5 (1...♗xg5? would lose the black queen to 2 ♕xf2 and 1...♔h8? 2 ♕f8 is mate) **2 ♕h5+ ♔g8 3 ♕e8+ ♔h7 Draw agreed**.

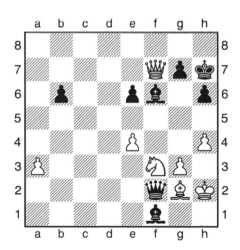

Knowing this important *perpetual-check* pattern may save you some miraculous half-points. A lone queen takes on an opposing queen and rook – and salvages a draw!

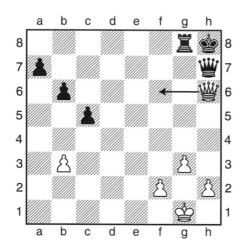

87a) White moves

Mi.Nikolić-G.Todorović
Belgrade (teams) 2009

Although a rook down, White can draw with a perpetual check.

1 ♕f6+ ♖g7 2 ♕d8+ Draw agreed.
There is no way for Black to escape the checks; e.g., 2...♕g8 3 ♕h4+ ♖h7 4 ♕f6+ ♕g7 5 ♕d8+. So the game is a draw.

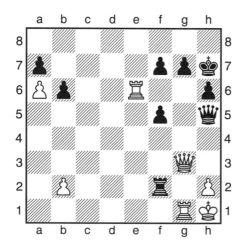

87b) Black moves

Svidler-V.Belov, Moscow 2003

White has an extra rook – and threatens mate in one. How was he swindled out of a win?

1...♖xh2+! 2 ♕xh2 Draw agreed.
Even though White is now *two* rooks ahead, it makes no difference: 2...♕f3+ sets up a perpetual check.

KNIGHT SACRIFICE PERPETUAL CLASSIC

This perpetual-check trick is well hidden. At precisely
the right moment, a surprise *knight check* forces
open the h-file, establishing the drawing formation.

88a) Black moves

Ha.van den Berg-Do.Klein, Dieren 2007

In this apparently lost position for Black,
a knight sacrifice saves the draw.

1...♘g3+! 2 hxg3 White must capture
with the pawn, as his queen is pinned at
the moment. 2...♕h5+ 3 ♕h2 ♕f3+ 4
♖g2 ♕d1+ 5 ♕g1 ♕h5+ Draw agreed.

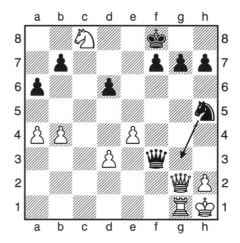

88b) White moves

Prusikin-Buhmann, Griesheim 2003

White was in difficulty and headed for
this position. What is the ingenious
drawing plan?

1 ♖d7! (to give access to the f6-square;
too early is 1 ♘g6+? ♖xg6) 1...♕xd7 2
♕f6+ ♕g7 3 ♘g6+! hxg6 4 ♕h4+ ♕h7
5 ♕f6+ ♖g7 6 ♕d8+ Draw agreed.

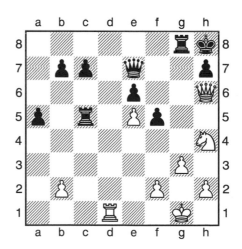

89 A QUEEN & KNIGHT PERPETUAL

Now for a useful *perpetual-check* pattern using queen and knight.

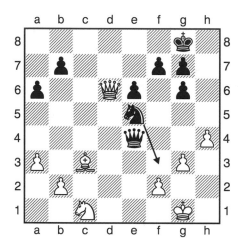

89a) Black moves

Elianov-Wang Hao, Sarajevo 2009

Black is a piece down – but his queen and knight are well placed for a *perpetual check*.

1...♘f3+ 2 ♔f1 Risking a discovered check is almost never advisable: 2 ♔h1? ♘xh4+ 3 ♔g1 ♕g2 mate. **2...♘h2+ Draw agreed**. On 3 ♔g1 ♘f3+ 4 ♔f1 ♘h2+, the checks continue.

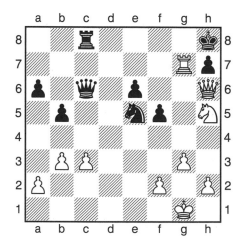

89b) Black moves

Kindermann-Wilder, Dortmund 1988

Black's king is cornered. How can he nevertheless save a draw by perpetual?

1...♘f3+ 2 ♔f1 ♘xh2+ 3 ♔g1 (if the king heads to the centre, White loses: 3 ♔e1? ♕xc3+ or 3 ♔e2? ♕f3+ 4 ♔e1 ♕xc3+) **3...♘f3+ 4 ♔f1 ♘h2+ 5 ♔g1 ♘f3+ Draw agreed**.

This handy formation has rescued many a bad endgame. The rook *restricts the enemy king* while the knight administers *perpetual check*. The key to this save is placing your rook on the correct square.

90a) White moves

M.Kislov-Vi.Bures, Olomouc 2003

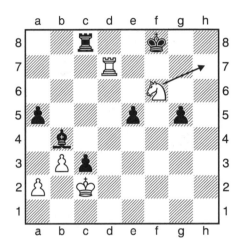

Although White is two pawns down, his rook and knight cooperate to give *perpetual check*.

1 ♘h7+ ♚e8 2 ♘f6+ ♚f8 3 ♘h7+ Draw agreed. There is no way for Black to escape the knight checks – 3...♚g8 4 ♘f6+ ♚h8? 5 ♖h7 is mate!

90b) White moves

Bany-Hawelko, Polish Ch, Bytom 1986

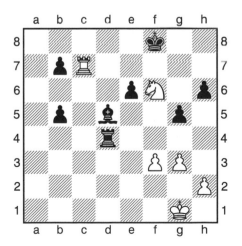

If 1 ♘h7+ ♚e8 2 ♘f6+ ♚d8, there is no perpetual. What subtle move saves the draw from this dubious position?

1 ♖d7! (setting up the key formation) **1...b4 2 ♘h7+ Draw agreed**. White draws by repeated checks: 2...♚e8 3 ♘f6+ ♚f8 4 ♘h7+.

SOMETHING OLD, SOMETHING NEW

Here we see two more saves using *perpetual check*. In the first, a familiar old motif saves the draw. In the second puzzle, you must tussle with a bizarre and original starting position.

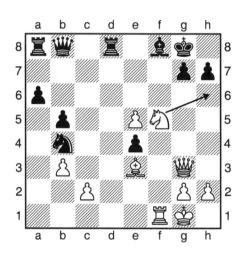

91a) White moves

Loskutov-Dzhangobegov, Moscow 2012

White is a rook down, but can draw with a standard perpetual-check defence.

1 ♘h6+ ♔h8 2 ♘f7+ ♔g8 3 ♘h6+ ♔h8 4 ♘f7+ ♔g8 5 ♘h6+ Draw. Black cannot escape the knight checks.

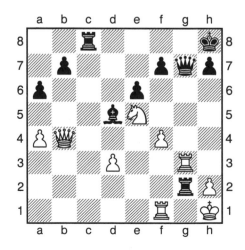

91b) White moves

Caruana-Van Wely, Amsterdam 2010

A crazy situation. If 1 ♖xg7 a discovered check wins for Black: 1...♖xg7+ 2 ♘f3 ♗xf3+ 3 ♖xf3 ♖c1+. So how does White draw?

1 ♘xf7+! ♔g8 (if 1...♕xf7?, 2 ♕d4+ with mate in two) **2 ♘h6+!** ♔h8 **3 ♘f7+ ♔g8 4 ♘h6+ Draw agreed**.

Tactical errors are more likely when players face unfamiliar piece- and pawn-formations. It pays to calculate variations especially carefully in unusual positions.

92a) White moves

Dearing-Talsma, British League 2011/12

A known opening trap – but who is tricking whom?

1 f4! Black resigns. 1...♘f3+ had been the plan. Too late, Black notices that 2 exf3! ♗xb2 3 ♕e2+ forks king and bishop. White's second move (doubling his pawns) is anti-positional and easily missed.

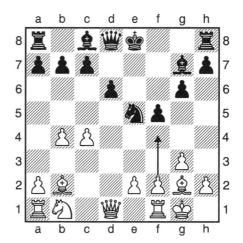

92b) Black moves

Babujian – Ter-Sahakian
Armenian Ch, Erevan 2012

A weird queenside configuration. What winning black move has White completely overlooked?

1...♕d2+! 2 ♕xd2 cxd2+ 3 ♔xd2 ♘e4+ 4 ♔e1 ♘xg5 and Black has won a piece.

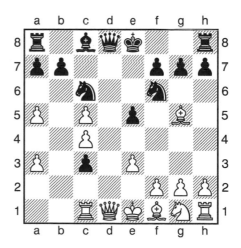

THE SLAV TRAP

Players of many levels fall for this trap, in which a black bishop move unexpectedly creates *two* threats. A white rook is attacked – plus the white queen is suddenly in danger.

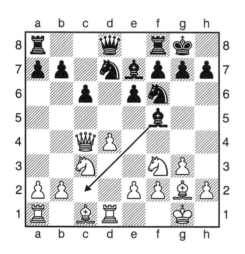

93a) Black moves

Opening Trap, Slav Defence

White has just played his rook to d1. A natural move – yet also a blunder.

1...♗c2! Now White's biggest problem is that 2...♘b6 threatens to trap the white queen! An escape-hole on a2 is urgently created. **2 a4 ♗xd1 3 ♘xd1** Black has won rook for bishop.

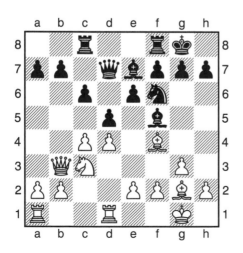

93b) Black moves

Schrittwieser-D.Hartl
Austrian League 2008/9

What strong two-move sequence does Black have in this position?

1...dxc4 2 ♕xc4 ♗c2! (threatening 3...b5, trapping the queen; White has no time to save his rook) **3 e4 ♗xd1** and Black wins rook for bishop.

104

DOUBLE TROUBLE

Discovered checks and *double checks* are powerful
tactical weapons. Slip one of these past your opponent,
and you might win right in the opening...

94a) White moves

Salai-T.Papatheodorou, Olomouc 2003

Black expects a recapture on c3, but instead learns the hard way about double
checks.

1 ♗g5++! Black resigns. White's move
is a *double check*. Black is in check from
both rook and bishop, so 1...♔e8 is
forced, after which White checkmates
with 2 ♖d8.

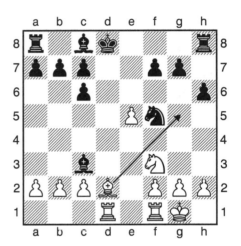

94b) White moves

Glek-Arkhipov, Russian Team Ch, Tomsk 2001

This grandmaster clash had a curious
finish. Can you find White's forced win?

1 ♘d6+ ♗xd6 (or 1...♔e7 2 ♕h5) **2
♕xd5! Black resigns**. White attacks
pieces on d6 and a8, and if 2...exd5 the
win is 3 exd6+, a *discovered check*, with
4 dxc7 to follow.

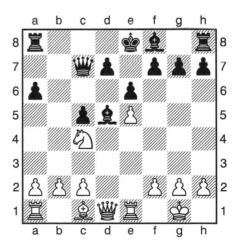

105

BALASHOV'S QUEEN BLUNDER

In 44 years of competitive chess, it was the shortest ever loss for Russian grandmaster Yuri Balashov. Black's queen gets trapped in just 12 moves – to a sneaky but known motif.

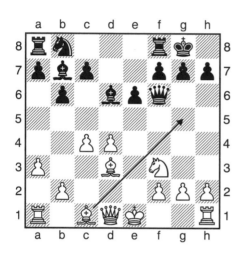

95a) White moves

Lugovoi-Balashov
Russian Ch, Krasnoiarsk 2003

This game started as a Nimzo-Indian Defence. The queen-trap idea that White now springs is familiar from other opening systems.

1 ♗g5 ♗xf3 2 ♕d2! Black resigns. His queen has been cleverly trapped – if 2...♕xd4, 3 ♗xh7+ ♔xh7 4 ♕xd4.

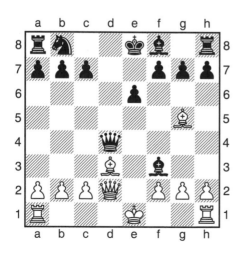

95b) White moves

Opening Trap, French Defence

The moves 1 e4 e6 2 d4 d5 3 ♘d2 dxe4 4 ♘xe4 ♗d7 5 ♘f3 ♗c6 6 ♗d3 ♘f6 7 ♘xf6+ ♕xf6? 8 ♗g5 ♗xf3 9 ♕d2 ♕xd4 reach the diagram position. How does White win from here?

10 ♗b5+ wins due to a discovered attack on the black queen.

A RIGHT-ROYAL
ENDGAME TACTIC

Queen and pawn endgames can sometimes take hours
to finish. So keep an eye out for this modest manoeuvre,
which can sometimes win in an instant.

96a) White moves

Blasko-E.Toth, Hungarian League 2005/6

Forget about capturing the b7-pawn –
the game can be ended at a stroke.

1 ♕g8! Black resigns. White's little
queen move traps the black king. Checkmate is coming with 2 ♕h8.

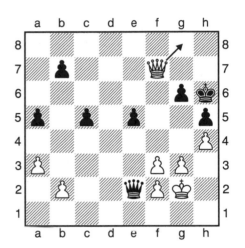

96b) White moves

Iv.Šarić-Stokke, Pula 2010

If you know the right manoeuvre, the
black position is not as solid as it seems.

1 ♕f7+ ♔h6 (or 1...♔h8 2 ♕xg6, winning) **2 ♕g8! Black resigns**. 2...♕a7
stops mate, but White liquidates to a
winning pawn endgame: 3 ♕h8+ ♕h7
4 ♕xh7+ ♔xh7 5 b4! axb4 6 a5.

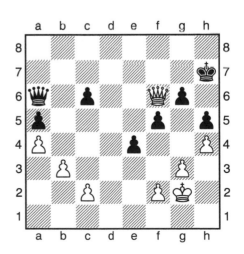

UPSIDE-DOWN CHESS

These two endgame puzzles – from opposite ends of the same New Zealand tournament hall – are linked by a common theme.

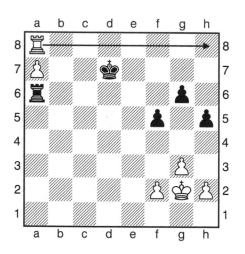

97a) White moves

Zulfić-A.Booth, Queenstown 2009

White showed impeccable technique in winning this game from the bottom boards.

1 ♖h8! A well-known skewer motif. White threatens to promote his pawn, and on 1...♖xa7, 2 ♖h7+ wins the black rook.

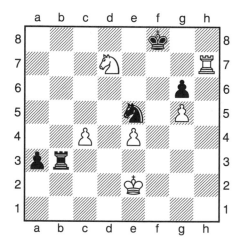

97b) Black moves

Smerdon-V.Mikhalevski, Queenstown 2009

This top-board clash was agreed drawn here. What hidden win had they missed?

1...♘xd7 2 ♖xd7 a2 3 ♖a7 (if 3 ♖d1, then 3...♖b1) **3...♖h3!** is the astonishing win. After **4 ♔d2** a familiar rook-skewer idea appears: **4...♖h1! 5 ♖xa2 ♖h2+** and next 6...♖xa2.

CONJURING UP A PASSED PAWN

A far-advanced pawn, near to promotion, is a potential game-winner. So take a close look at these two high-level puzzles. A passed pawn materializes on the sixth rank, as if by magic...

98a) White moves

Swiercz-Lomsadze
European Ch, Plovdiv 2012

"Where is the passed pawn?" A Polish grandmaster waves his tactical wand...

1 Rxh7! Very nice. If 1...Kxh7 the new passed pawn is decisive: 2 Rd7+ Kg8 3 h7+ Kh8 4 Bf6+. **1...Rxa2 2 Rdd7 Black resigns**. Mate by 3 Bf6 and 4 Rh8 is imminent.

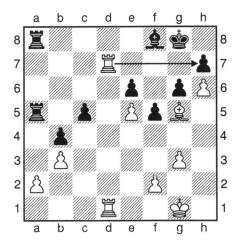

98b) Black moves

Kramnik-Anand
World Ch match game 5, Bonn 2008

Some sorcery from the World Champion himself. What happened next?

1...Ne3! 2 fxe3 fxe3 White resigns. There is no satisfactory defence to the threat of 3...e2 next move.

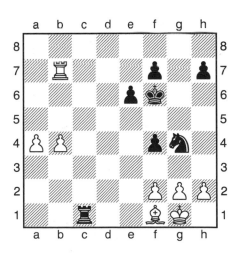

DON'T TRY THIS AT HOME

Patterns are a great help in spotting tactics. But occasionally a move is so extraordinary it can only be found by calculation or inspiration. Don't expect to copy these originals – they are one-offs!

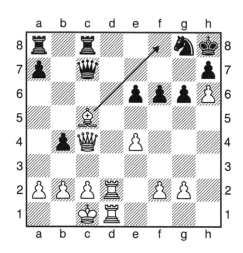

99a) White moves

D.Mastrovasilis-Short
European Team Ch, Porto Carras 2011

A freak move catches out one of the smartest grandmasters on the circuit.

1 ♗f8! ♕xc4 (if 1...♖xf8, 2 ♕xc7 or 1...♘e7 2 ♗g7+ ♔g8 3 ♕xe6 mate) **2 ♗g7 checkmate**.

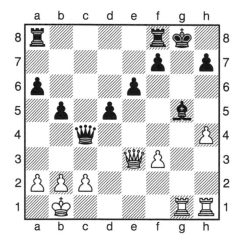

99b) Black moves

Y.Vovk-Shishkin, Odessa 2006

Consider Black's bishop on g5 – pinned, and under attack from *three* white pieces. Now work out how Black wins in one move – and the bishop survives.

1...♕f1+! **White resigns**. After 2 ♖xf1 ♗xe3 Black remains a piece ahead.

AND IT'S GOOD KNIGHT FROM HIM

We end with a motif that might catch anyone by surprise...

100a) Black moves

Berset-Skembris, Basle 2012

White has not yet castled, but it is not obvious the omission will cost him the game.

1...♘f5! White resigns. The trapped queen can be saved only at the cost of a piece.

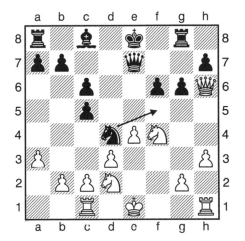

100b) White moves

Korchnoi-Smirin, Odessa (rapidplay) 2007

How did Viktor Korchnoi, 76 years old, outfox his opponent in this rapid game?

1 ♘c1! Black resigns. The backwards knight move wrong-foots Grandmaster Smirin. Black's rook on e8 is twice-attacked, but after 1...♖xe1, 2 ♘xd3! will win a piece.

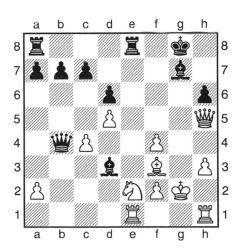

MISSION IMPOSSIBLE

Test One

In this test, you are on your own, without illustrative examples to guide you. Sometimes the solution will be a single move, perhaps winning a pawn or a piece. Other times it may be a checkmating theme, lasting three or more moves.

If you need a hint, you can look up the related 'Puzzle' from the main section of the book.

Solutions start on page 118.

Target Scores

Award yourself 1 point for each combination correctly solved (without using the hints).

28-30	International Master standard
24-27	Tournament-strength player
20-23	Excellent pattern recognition
15-19	Promising tactical ability
10-14	Average
5-9	More practice needed
0-4	Try Sudoku

CONJURING UP A
PASSED PAWN

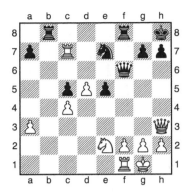

1) Black wins
Hint: see Puzzle 69

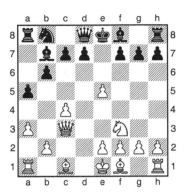

2) Black wins
Hint: see Puzzle 62

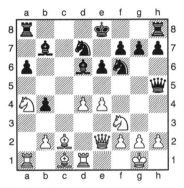

3) Black wins
Hint: see Puzzle 79

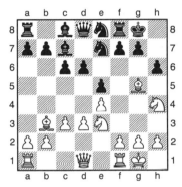

4) White wins
Hint: see Puzzle 6

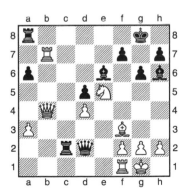

5) Black wins
Hint: see Puzzle 70

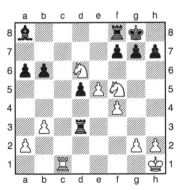

6) White wins
Hint: see Puzzle 49

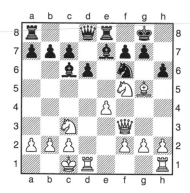

7) White wins
Hint: see Puzzle 16

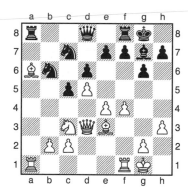

8) Black wins
Hint: see Puzzle 44

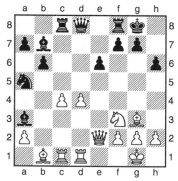

9) White wins
Hint: see Puzzle 1

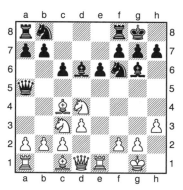

10) White wins
Hint: see Puzzle 11

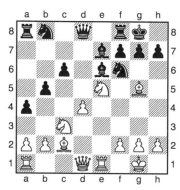

11) White wins
Hint: see Puzzle 4

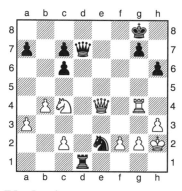

12) Black wins
Hint: see Puzzle 47

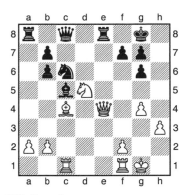

13) White wins
Hint: see Puzzle 8

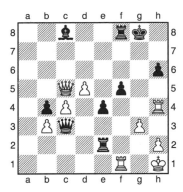

14) White wins
Hint: see Puzzle 25

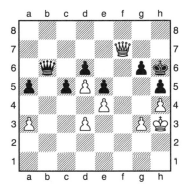

15) White wins
Hint: see Puzzle 96

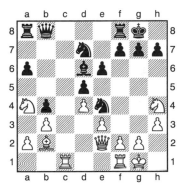

16) Black wins
Hint: see Puzzle 29

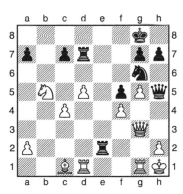

17) Black draws
Hint: see Puzzle 87

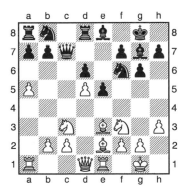

18) White wins
Hint: see Puzzle 62

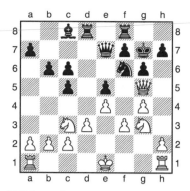

19) White wins
Hint: see Puzzle 33

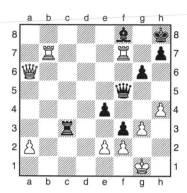

20) Black wins
Hint: see Puzzle 73

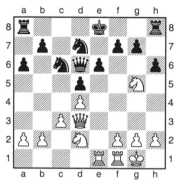

21) White wins
Hint: see Puzzle 60

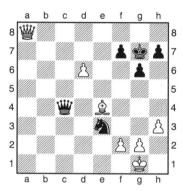

22) Black wins
Hint: see Puzzle 48

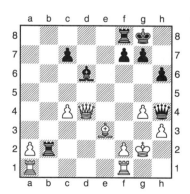

23) Black wins
Hint: see Puzzle 9

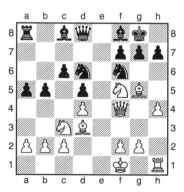

24) White wins
Hint: see Puzzle 15

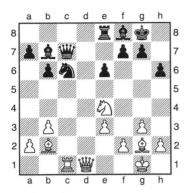

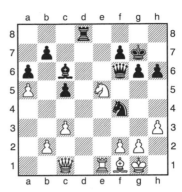

25) White wins
Hint: see Puzzle 19

26) Black wins
Hint: see Puzzle 40

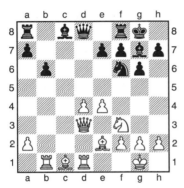

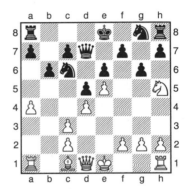

27) Black wins
Hint: see Puzzle 35

28) White wins
Hint: see Puzzle 41

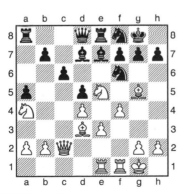

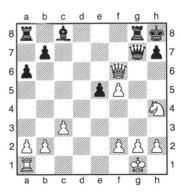

29) White wins
Hint: see Puzzle 82

30) White draws
Hint: see Puzzle 88

Solutions to Test One (positions 1-30)

1. 1...♕xf2+! White resigns, since 2 ♖xf2 ♖b1+ leads to a quick checkmate (M.Pap-B.Maksimović, Serbian League 2006).

2. 1...♗b4! White resigns, due to 2 axb4 axb4 3 ♕xb4 ♖xa1 (A.Schmied-Schlindwein, Untergrombach 2003).

3. 1...♗xh2+! wins a pawn (Berczes-Galyas, Budapest 2002).

4. 1 ♗xe7 ♕xe7 2 ♘g6 forks queen and rook (Bergez-Sebag, Creon 2000).

5. 1...♕xf2+! Black resigns, due to the coming checkmate after 2 ♖xf2 ♖c1+ 3 ♖f1 ♗e3+ (Szakolczai-Okara, Budapest 2006).

6. 1 ♘e7+ ♔h8 2 ♘xf7+! Black resigns, as 2...♖xf7 3 ♖c8+ ♖f8 4 ♖xf8 is mate (Lepot-C.Peyre, Pau 2008).

7. 1 ♗xh6! wins a pawn due to 1...gxh6 2 ♕g3+ (Mrdja-Mrksić, Crikvenica 2008).

8. 1...♖xa6! 2 ♖xa6 c4 White resigns, as the *zwischenzug* wins a piece (Decoster-Tjiam, Belgian League 2011/12).

9. 1 ♕d3 Black resigns as both mate on h7 and the bishop on a3 are threatened (V.Khachatrian-Sholkovsky, Yuzhny 2009).

10. 1 ♘xe6! fxe6 2 ♖xe6 wins two pawns, as White threatens a discovered check (Kubit-B.Andrejczuk, Polanica Zdroj 2005).

11. 1 ♕d3 g6 2 ♘xg6! hxg6 3 ♖xe6! wins a pawn, as 3...fxe6 4 ♕xg6+ leads to mate (Prikhodko-V.Lazutin, Dimitrovgrad 2010).

12. 1...♖h1+! Black resigns, as 2 ♔xh1 ♕d1+ 3 ♔h2 ♕g1 is mate (P.Hofbauer-Kuba, Austrian League 1998/9).

13. 1 ♘f6+! gxf6 2 ♕xg6+ gives White a winning attack (Jo.Novotny-Rakus, Czech League 2005/6).

14. 1 ♖g4+! mates or wins the black queen (Ghorbani-Niknaddaf, Iranian Ch, Mashad 2003).

15. 1 ♕g8! ♕c7 2 ♕h8+ ♕h7 3 ♕f8+ ♕g7 4 ♕xd6 winning a pawn (Rusev-A.Asenov, Rouse 2004).

16. 1...♗h2+ 2 ♔h1 ♗g3! 3 ♘f3 ♗xf2! 4 ♖xf2 ♘g3+ and the white queen was lost (Nylen-R.Bator, Swedish League 2006/7).

17. 1...♖xh2+! Draw agreed, as 2 ♕xh2 ♕f3+ starts a *perpetual check* (Jobava-Volkov, Moscow 2008).

18. 1 ♗b6! axb6 2 axb6 ♕xb6 3 ♖xa8 wins an exchange for a pawn (O.Orel-Babnik, Slovenian Ch, Skofja Loka 2000).

19. 1 ♘h5+! wins a piece (R.Anton-B.Bercaru, Romanian Women's Ch, Eforie Nord 2009).

20. 1...♖c1+ 2 ♔h2 ♖h1+! **White resigns** (L.Spasov-J.Torralba, Manresa 1996).

21. 1 ♖xe6+! fxe6 2 ♕g6+ ♔d8 (or 2...♔e7 3 ♕xg7+) **3 ♘f7+** forks king and queen (C.Singer-Grawe, Munich 2011).

22. 1...♕c1+ 2 ♔h2 ♘f1+ 3 ♔g1 ♘g3+! 4 ♔h2 ♘e2 5 h4 ♕f4+ **White resigns** (Harika Dronavalli-Melia, World Girls' Ch, Erevan 2007).

23. 1...♕g3+ 2 ♔h1 ♕h2 mate (Je.van der Ende-Baselmans, Dutch Under-11 Ch, Waalwijk 2011).

24. 1 ♘h6+ ♔h8 2 ♕xd6! ♕xd6 3 ♘xf7+ ♔g8 4 ♘xd6 wins a pawn (Sinka-Ortel, Hungarian League 2006/7).

25. 1 ♘f6+! gxf6 2 ♕g4+ (full marks also for 2 ♗xf6) **2...♔h7 3 ♗xf6 ♘e5 4 ♗e4+!** **Black resigns** (Reschke-Klüners, Bad Zwesten 2003).

26. 1...♗xg2! 2 ♗xg2 ♕g5 3 ♘g4 ♘e2+! **White resigns**, as 4 ♖xe2 ♕xc1+ wins the white queen (Mikac-Bednarich, Nova Gorica 2001).

27. 1...♘xe4! 2 ♕xe4 ♗f5 skewers the white queen and rook (Jedynak-B.Grabarczyk, Poraj 1997).

28. 1 ♗h6! wins material in view of 1...gxh5 2 ♗g7 or 1...♘xh6 2 ♘f6+ (Ivanović-Trikaliotis, Corfu 1990).

29. 1 ♗xf6 ♗xf6 2 ♘xd7 ♘xd7 (if 2...♕xd7, 3 ♘b6 forks queen and rook) **3 ♗xh7+** wins a pawn (C.Flear-Y.Cavusoglu, European Women's Ch, Istanbul 2003).

30. 1 ♘g6+! hxg6 2 ♕h4+ ♕h7 3 ♕f6+ and White draws by perpetual check: **3...♖g7 4 ♕d8+ ♕g8 5 ♕h4+ ♖h7 6 ♕f6+**, etc. (G.Schuchardt-Habibi, Kassel 1999).

BACKWARD PAWN

119

MISSION IMPOSSIBLE

Test Two

In a serious tournament game, you would be using a chess clock. So in Test Two there is an additional challenge: time! Your mission – should you choose to accept it – is to try to solve each puzzle **within just five minutes**.

If you need a hint, you can look up the related 'Puzzle' from the main section of the book.

Solutions start on page 126.

Target Scores (without using hints)

Award yourself **2 points** for each combination correctly solved *in five minutes or less*. If you take longer, but still get the right solution, award yourself **1 point**.

54-60	International Master standard
45-53	Tournament-strength player
38-44	Excellent pattern recognition
26-37	Promising tactical ability
14-25	Average
7-13	More practice needed
0-6	Try Sudoku

A DELIGHTFUL DECOY

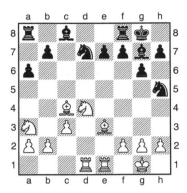

31) White wins
Hint: see Puzzle 13

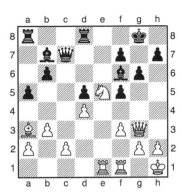

32) White wins
Hint: see Puzzle 45

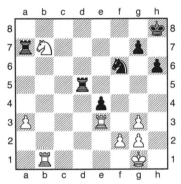

33) Black wins
Hint: see Puzzle 68

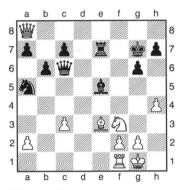

34) White wins
Hint: see Puzzle 23

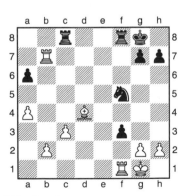

35) Black wins
Hint: see Puzzle 72

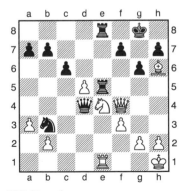

36) White wins
Hint: see Puzzle 37

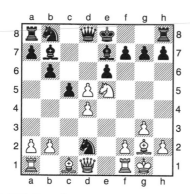

37) White wins
Hint: see Puzzle 61

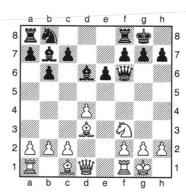

38) White wins
Hint: see Puzzle 95

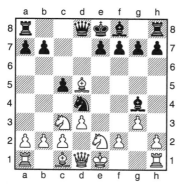

39) Black wins
Hint: see Puzzle 58

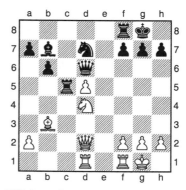

40) White wins
Hint: see Puzzle 14

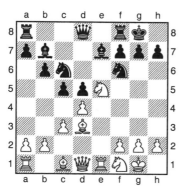

41) White wins
Hint: see Puzzle 42

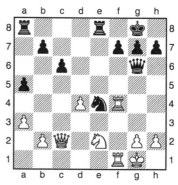

42) Black wins
Hint: see Puzzle 46

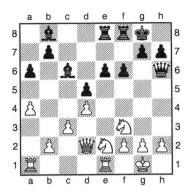

43) Black wins
Hint: see Puzzle 78

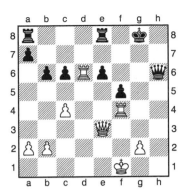

44) White wins
Hint: see Puzzle 64

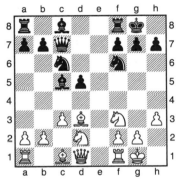

45) Black wins
Hint: see Puzzle 7

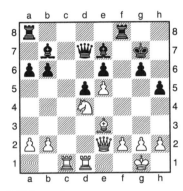

46) White wins
Hint: see Puzzle 43

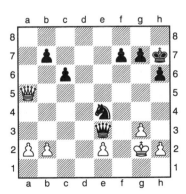

47) White draws
Hint: see Puzzle 85

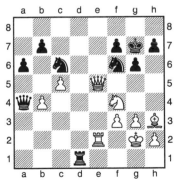

48) White wins
Hint: see Puzzle 34

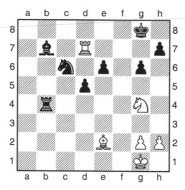

49) White draws
Hint: see Puzzle 90

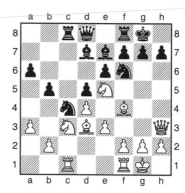

50) White wins
Hint: see Puzzle 78

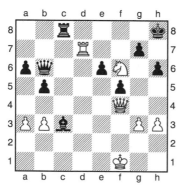

51) White wins
Hint: see Puzzle 52

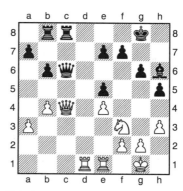

52) White wins
Hint: see Puzzle 75

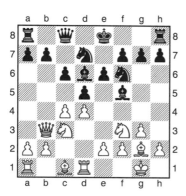

53) Black wins
Hint: see Puzzle 93

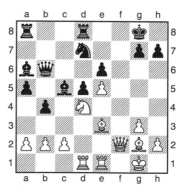

54) White wins
Hint: see Puzzle 10

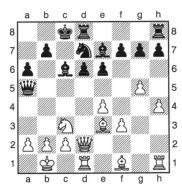

55) White wins
Hint: see Puzzle 66

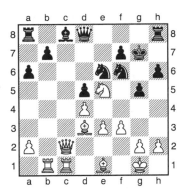

56) White wins
Hint: see Puzzle 30

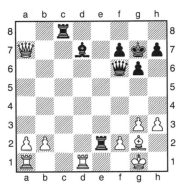

57) Black wins
Hint: see Puzzle 76

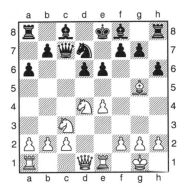

58) White wins
Hint: see Puzzle 59

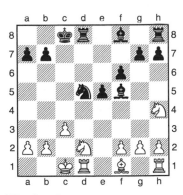

59) Black wins
Hint: see Puzzle 51

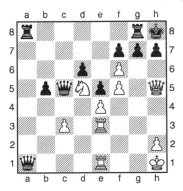

60) White wins
Hint: see Puzzle 57

Solutions to Test Two (positions 31-60)

31. 1 ♘e6! fxe6 2 ♗xe6+ ♖f7 3 ♗xd7 and White has won a pawn (Altounian-D.Gurevich, USA Ch, St Louis 2010).

32. 1 ♘g4! ♕c6 (if 1...♕xg3 White has a *zwischenzug*: 2 ♘xf6+ ♔g7 3 hxg3 ♔xf6 4 ♗e7+) **2 ♘xf6+ ♕xf6 3 ♗e7** wins the exchange (Je.Rotstein-Sandmann, Bad Bertrich 2001).

33. 1...♖xb7! 2 ♖xb7 ♖d1+ 3 ♔h2 ♘g4+ 4 ♔h3 ♘xf2+ 5 ♔h4 ♖h1 checkmate (Holt-Panchanathan, Berkeley 2011).

34. 1 ♗h6+! ♔xh6 2 ♕f8+ ♖g7 3 ♘xe5 leaves the black king stranded and exposed. The game ended **3...♕e6 4 ♕f4+ g5 5 hxg5+ ♖xg5 6 ♘f7+ Black resigns** (Prusikin-Ftačnik, German League 2002/3).

35. 1...♘xd4 2 cxd4 f2+! 3 ♔h1 (if 3 ♖xf2, then 3...♖c1+) **3...♖c1! White resigns** (S.Nedeljković-G.Szilagyi, Hungary vs Yugoslavia, Budapest 1957).

36. 1 ♘f6+ ♔h8 2 ♗g7+! ♔xg7 3 ♘xe8+ ♖xe8 4 ♕xd4+ ♘xd4 5 ♖xe8 with a winning endgame for White (E.Ju-Ippolito, Parsippany 2007).

37. 1 ♘xf7! ♔xf7 2 dxe6+ ♔g8 3 ♗xb7 is good for White (Disconzi da Silva-E.Espinoza, Rio de Janeiro 2003).

38. 1 ♗g5 ♗xf3 2 ♕d2! Black resigns (Welling-Sabel, Dresden 2003).

39. 1...♕xd5! wins, because 2 ♘xd5 ♘f3+ 3 ♔f1 ♗h3 is mate (Gurgenidze-Kotov, Erevan 1955).

40. 1 ♘e6! fxe6 2 dxe6 ♕xd2 3 ♖xd2 and the threat of a discovered check gives White a winning position (Grigoriadis-F.Stamos, Nikea 2010).

41. 1 ♗a6! and White wins material (S.Perić-D.Martinez Martin, Mondariz 1988).

42. 1...♘g3! White resigns, as on 2 ♕xg6 the *zwischenzug* 2...♘xe2+ wins a knight (Kohlrusz-G.Horvath, Hungarian League 2003/4).

43. 1...♗xh2+! wins a pawn (Cornejo-Lafuente, Callao 2007).

44. 1 ♖g4+! Black resigns. The black queen is lost to a *discovered attack* as 1...♔h7 is met by 2 ♖d7+ (M.Kislov-An.Dekker, Trinec 1998).

45. 1...♗xh3! wins a pawn, as 2 gxh3 ♕g3+ 3 ♔h1 ♕xh3+ 4 ♔g1 ♘g4 would give Black two pawns and a decisive attack for the bishop (R.Frosch-Kosten, Austrian League 2007/8). Score also if you chose the equally thematic 1...♕g3, which also leaves White in deep trouble.

46. 1 ♖c7! Black resigns as 1...♕xc7 2 ♘xe6+ forks king and queen (Kr.Georgiev-Al.Spasov, Sunny Beach 2005).

47. 1 ♕f5+ ♔g8 2 ♕c8+ Draw agreed, as perpetual check is coming (D.Fridman-Melia, Caleta 2011).

48. 1 ♞h5+! gxh5 2 ♛g5+ ♚f8 3 ♛xf6 leaves the black position a wreck, and after **3...♛a1 4 ♛h6+ Black resigned** (McNab-Noyce, Dublin Zonal 1993).

49. 1 ♞f6+ ♚f8 2 ♞xh7+ ♚e8 3 ♞f6+ ♚f8 4 ♞h7+ ♚e8 5 ♞f6+ ♚f8 6 ♞h7+ Draw (Pa.Dimitrov-Okhotnik, Bled 2008).

50. 1 ♞xd5! wins due to 1...exd5 2 ♞xd7 and if 2...♛xd7, then 3 ♝xh7+ ♚h8 4 ♝f5+ (P.Frydman-Vidmar, Ujpest 1934).

51. 1 ♛xh6+! Black resigns (Rozentalis-Kantsler, Israeli League 2011/12).

52. 1 ♜d8+! Black resigns (O.Orel-Hanley, Aschach 2004).

53. 1...dxc4 2 ♛xc4 ♝c2! wins rook for bishop, as 3 ♜d2 fails to 3...♞b6, trapping the white queen (Gereben-V.Ragozin, Budapest vs Moscow 1949).

54. 1 ♞xe6! ♝xe3 2 ♛xe3 (also 2 ♜xe3) and the black centre collapses, since 2...♛xe6 3 ♝xd5 pins the queen (Kolomensky-O.Belova, Samara 2011).

55. 1 ♞d5! Black resigns, as 1...♛xd2 2 ♞xe7+ wins a piece (Papa-C.Astengo, Biel 2003).

56. 1 ♝g6! is strong as the black f7-pawn is lost next move; e.g., 1...♜f8 2 ♝xf7! ♜xf7 3 ♛g6+ (Razuvaev-C.Pesantes, Cienfuegos 1975).

57. 1...♜c7! (based on 2 ♛xc7 ♛xf2+) **2 ♛d4 ♜e1+! White resigns** (G.Vojino-vić-Kožul, Bosnian Team Ch, Neum 2002).

58. 1 ♞xe6! is crushing – on the recapture 1...fxe6 Black will get mated starting with 2 ♛h5+ (Opening Trap, Sicilian Defence).

59. 1...♞xc3! 2 ♞xf5 ♞xd1 White resigns, due to 3 ♚xd1 ♝b4, winning the knight on d2 (Tsifanskaya-Shavtvaladze, Ikaros 2002).

60. 1 ♛xh7+! Black resigns (K.J.E.Lee-A.Marley, High Wycombe 2012).

PICKING OFF THE PIECES

Other chess books
produced by ...

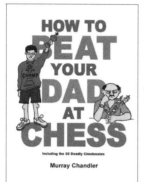

HOW TO BEAT YOUR DAD AT CHESS
(Chandler) **128 pages**   **$16.95 £12.50**

"Fun to read for players of any age or any strength" – **Lubosh Kavalek, WASHINGTON POST**

"Don't let the title fool you, overall this is a great book that will teach many important winning patterns" – **Andy May, NSGCHESS.COM**

"The charm of this book is that every position is a deadly checkmate ... simple but extremely instructional. Great fun" – **Bernard Hannison, CHESS POST**

CHESS TACTICS FOR KIDS
(Chandler) **128 pages**   **$16.95 £12.50**

"Though there are many, many tactics books available, I've not seen one that is so thoughtfully laid out and written so well for the junior player" – **Daniel Lucas, KIDCHESS.COM**

"As a teacher of scholastic/junior players, I have long wished for a comprehensive yet brief and inexpensive guide to chess tactics ... finally a work that fits the bill" – **Bill Whited, CHESS COUNTRY**

"When you go deeper into the book, you'll find tricks that even grandmasters could miss" – **Stuart Solomon, CHESSVILLE**

CHESS OPENINGS FOR KIDS
(Watson & Burgess) **128 pages**   **$16.95 £12.50**

"...provides a very succinct overview of the main openings and the ideas behind them" – **Luke McShane, NEW IN CHESS**

"Introduces kids to the otherwise bewildering array of names and variations of the openings. Along the way, it discusses every significant principle of strategy" – **Cecil Rosner, WINNIPEG FREE PRESS**

"All major chess openings plus all the strategies ... a lovely easy learning openings book!" – **John Elburg, CHESSBOOKS.NL**